TOK

Diaspora Dialogues
presents

TOK

book 2
Helen Walsh, editor

Zephyr Press

Zephyr Press
170 Bloor Street West, Suite 804
Toronto, Ontario M5S 1T9
www.zephyrpress.ca

Library and Archives Canada Cataloguing in Publication

   Tok : diaspora dialogues / Helen Walsh, editor.

ISBN 978-0-9734112-4-9

   1. Short stories, Canadian (English)—Ontario—Toronto.
2. Canadian poetry (English)—Ontario—Toronto.
3. Canadian fiction (English)—21st century.
4. Toronto (Ont.)—Literary collections. I. Walsh, Helen, 1965–

PS8237.T6T54 2006   C810.8'032713541   C2006-902670-X

Book design and composition by The Office of Gilbert Li
Copyediting by Madeline Koch
Cover images from the series *Soles*, by TEK
Printed and bound in Canada by Transcontinental Inc.

The paper used in this book contains 100% post-consumer fibre,
is acid-free, processed chlorine free, EcoLogo-certified, and was
manufactured with biogas energy.

The Conditions
Necessary
for Revolution
by Lawrence Hill

Ella can't be bought with Cracker Jacks and Coke. Itching in her woollen tights and longing to peel them off, unbuckle her Lady Oxfords and throw the whole lot of Sunday clothes down down down on the conductor's head, she refuses to touch Mother's peace offerings.

"Go ahead, have some," Mother says.

"I don't feel like it."

"There will be consequences if I hear any L, A & S," Mother says.

She is talking about Lip, Attitude and Sass. According to Mother and the members of the fur coat club—Ella's private term for the Ladies' Church Auxiliary—L, A & S threaten western civilization no less than communism and atheism, combined.

Down on the stage, the first violinists are warming up. They sound like ten cats in heat. Ella refuses to look at Mother. She contemplates the conditions necessary for revolution. They are all present in her life.

First of all, there is struggle. Before the sun rose this very morning, Mother had placed her alarm clock—ringing like an overcaffeinated town crier—directly on Ella's pillow. All this to make Ella get out of bed so Mother could braid her hair in time for the eight o'clock church service. If Ella could go back in time to slap two people upside the head, she knows exactly who she would hunt down: the inventor of braids and the moron who scheduled church on Sundays. Sunday is a perfectly good no-school day. What a waste.

And second, there is alienation. Once she was braided, strait-jacketed into her Sunday best and warned not to fight with her brother, Ella had to endure an entire hour in the pews. What fun was church if she couldn't torture her brother? *I am alienated from my mother,* Ella muttered to herself, *and alienated from all church goers. I belong to some other family, race or nation. I am an alien, pure and simple, and cannot endure church indefinitely.*

That morning, Reverend Horace Fullerlove, windbag of the world, must have awakened thinking he was related to the late Martin Luther King, Jr. He started his sermon with a whisper. But it didn't take long to work himself up to hyperventilation at the pulpit. Mother, who espoused erect carriage and breathing through the diaphragm, exhaled in disgust when five ladies bounced out of their pews, had their moment of ecstasy with Jesus and fainted into the arms of church deacons.

"They're not fooling anybody," Mother whispered to Ella, trying to get on her good side.

Ella refused to look at Mother in church, the same way she's refusing to acknowledge her now. Church was bad enough. But being taken straight to Massey Hall and imprisoned in Seat 6, Row C, Second Balcony will drive Ella over the top. This will be her catalyst—a word Ella learned last week from Miss Meeks, who said that anger, like kindling, will wait until somebody lights a match. Anger, said her teacher, is perfectly happy to wait for years.

Mother lied to the people—the people being Ella and her brother—and she will pay for her crime. Even Walt has shown rumblings of discontent, and has asked Ella if it is possible to fire one's own mother. Walt has a decent heart, but he is a proletariat through and through. He will be lucky to sell his own labour. He will never become a leader of the masses. He will not even make it into Ella's school for the intellectually gifted. For that boy, there will be no special classes about the theory of revolution. In his hands, a book is best used as a missile.

"No," Ella had to tell him, "you can't fire your mother when your father has walked out."

Firing is out, but a general uprising has the support of the masses. From Ella, there will be no more model behaviour. She might even throw a geometry test and bring home a C. Ella will grant no more opportunities for Mother to spout off to all her ermine-hatted friends, who also have taken their kids straight from church: "She brings home straight As and is loved by her teachers, unlike that brother of hers, who is heading to hell on a go-cart if he keeps it up."

Mother passes the Cracker Jacks over Ella's lap to Walt.

"Don't stain your tie," Mother tells him.

When Mother turns to speak to her friend, Ella hisses at her brother. "You're eating from the hand that oppresses you."

"Shuddup, puddin'!" he says.

"Mother, he called me puddin," Ella says.

Mother turns her face to the side. Her brown lips tighten. A ridge darkens between her eyebrows. "Walt, I warned you about calling her that. Don't provoke me."

There must be many oppressed people, and they must have a leader. This was another necessary condition, Miss Meeks told the class. She was explaining the theory of revolution, as proposed by a German who died ages ago. He was a bearded white guy who looked like a grandfather.

The time is right for Ella to rise up. The concert program promises six Sunday events to introduce children to the classics. Above and beyond all else, Mother must not entertain any thought of returning to this mausoleum of oak seats and balustrades that creak and shift and smell of popcorn butter and threaten at every moment to collapse from the accumulated onslaught of a hundred years of violas and French horns. Collapse is what they should do, right onto the black music stands below. Mother will rue the hour of the unpardonable lie she had made this morning, while they were leaving the sanctuary of the African Methodist Episcopal Church.

"I'm taking you somewhere very special," Mother said.

"Can we just go home?" Walt said, sliding toward the aisle and drumming the beat of *You're Feisty*, a cool rap song Ella recognized from the Michie Mee & L.A. Luv record *Jamaican Funk: Canadian Style*. At home, Walt and Ella were allowed to listen to rap records, but only after Mother vetted them. Mother didn't permit rap songs that used four-letter words or that treated women like slabs of meat. The slabs of meat rule, yeah, okay, but the four-letter word business had stunned Ella. It had never occurred to her that her mother knew the words, or understood what they meant. Prior to the warning about four-letter words, the only bad word that Ella thought her mother knew was the N-word. You were not allowed to say it, period, and Mother had already written to the makers of the *Canadian Oxford Dictionary*, requesting that the word be deleted from the next edition. Poor Mother. Little did she know that these days, even white kids were calling each other *nigger*.

"Walt, stop tapping on that pew," Mother said. "And no, we're not going straight home. But you'll love it, where we're going. It's a surprise."

"What kind of surprise?" Ella said.

"A musical surprise. You'll hear music that you absolutely adore."

"Do you adore this music we're going to hear?" Walt said.

"It is heavenly music," Mother said.

"D'ja hear that?" Walt said to Ella. "Mother likes the stuff she's taking us to. Boy, I can't wait."

Walt wasn't a complete retard. He was just a boy. And as a boy, he had his limitations. One of them was a failure to grasp that you never ever, ever used sarcasm on Mother if you were within arm's reach.

Ella heard the whistle of Mother's palm on Walt's cheek. It was a ten out of ten, that slap. The kind, Mother liked to say, that would send you three days into the next week.

Walt pivoted so that Mother couldn't see his eyes grow wet, but Ella saw it. She saw it perfectly. A condition of the downtrodden.

"You will enjoy this music!" Mother said. "Do you understand? You will thank me for the experience."

Mother had a tear in her eye. This was something that Ella did not understand about adults. They could slap you in one moment and offer Cracker Jacks in the next. Mother's voice wore that timbre that meant *I can't believe you don't love me for all that I sacrifice for you.* Mother sulked as they walked to the car. Maybe, Ella thought, this would be good. Maybe it would be great music, right up there with Michie Mee.

Well, it isn't. It hasn't started yet, but Ella already hates it. She and Walt will have to listen to violins. The program says it will be the Adagio in F Major from Bach's Brandenburg Concerto #1, followed by Vivaldi's Concerto in D Major. *The Vivaldi Concerto is a bright piece whose first movement shows a delightful ambivalence of rhythm and whose finale is an extrovert moto perpetuo for the violins of the orchestra. A master of baroque music, Antonio Lucio Vivaldi wrote 550 concertos.* As far as Ella is concerned, that's 549 too many.

According to Miss Meeks, the bearded German said people won't act up until they feel downtrodden. Ella knows she is oppressed, but Walt must feel it too. The revolution will be lost without his cooperation.

"Ouch!" she cries, loud enough that the president of the women's church auxiliary, who sits to Mother's left, looks on. "Mother, Walt pinched me. OUCH! He stepped on my toe."

Walt's lip drops. "Did not," he stutters.

He ought to know it's no use. Mother reaches across Ella, who leans back to accommodate her, grabs Walt's tie with her left hand and wags her right index finger.

"No more highjinks," she says.

The orchestra begins to play. Mother sits upright and places her hand on the armrest beside Ella. It smells of hand lotion. Ella glances down quickly. She can barely detect the lighter band of brown skin once covered by the wedding ring.

"Listen to the oboes, darling," Mother says.

Swinging from slapping to sweet talking is a sure sign that her mother is cracking up. Each extra day that she goes on living without Father, and suspects that her own fur-coat friends are gossiping about how the new woman is young enough to be Father's daughter, Mother holds the reins more firmly. And that is a tactical mistake. Dogs on leashes are more likely to bite.

Conscious of her brother's stillness, Ella lets a minute pass.

"Why'd you do that?" Walt finally whispers.

Ellen cups her mouth and turns it towards her brother. "She believes anything I say, doesn't she?"

"It's not fair."

"Well, if you don't do what I say, I'll tell her you pinched me again."

While Walt chews that over, Ella listens to the fading oboes. There's a long pause. Pages rustle. Bach's over. Thank God for that. Must be Vivaldi next. *Vivaldi.* Ridiculous. The name sounds like hair gel. The guy has been dead and gone for like a quarter of a millennium so isn't it time to move on?

Maybe the program will distract Ella from her misery. Great. The first page looks like a textbook. On the second page, there is a diagram under the heading, *The Parts of the Violin.* Each part is named. Scroll. Tuning pegs. Neck. Bridge. Fine tuners. F-holes. You've got to be kidding. *F-holes*? Adults come up with most inane words precisely when they are trying to kill any possibility of laughter. Just a week earlier, Ella shut the dictionary when her mother came up to see what she had been reading. Secretly, she had been searching for the definition of "fart." *A minor explosion between the legs.*

"What were you looking up, dear?" Mother said.

"Fascism."

The conductor jabs his rod at the second violinists, who start sawing with their bows. They make a shimmering noise. They create the expectancy of more. For a millisecond, they speak to Ella. She imagines them saying, *Something good could happen today if you apply a little elbow grease.* But they breeze right by Ella and egg on the first violinists. They demand to be led, to be armed, to wreak havoc and chaos in the swirl of sound. Ella kind of likes it.

Now the first violinists kick in. They dig their chins into wooden instruments and start sawing madly, shimmering, shimmering, poking at a high note, dropping back down to join the shimmering, poking up and up again, kicking everybody else's butt in the orchestra.

"Now," Ella whispers to Walt.

"Now what?"

"Tell her I don't look too good. Tell her I'm feverish."

"Mother," Walt says, leaning across Ella.

"Shh."

"Mother, it's too hot in here. Ella's sick. She's feverish."

Ella shuts her eyes. She feels a cool hand on her forehead.

"Ella. Open your eyes."

Ella knows how to make her eyelids flutter when she opens them halfway. She's been working on that one for a while, alone in her bedroom. Ella has Mother exactly where she wants her. Solicitous. Unsuspecting. Weak.

"Are you all right?" Mother whispers.

"Yes," Ella mumbles.

"Good. Sit up then. Be silent. Isn't this exciting?"

Ella nods.

The first violins go, la la la la LA LA LA LA do do do do DO DO DO DO DOOOOO LA LA LA LA DOOOO DO DO DO DO. The second violins echo them, the first violins dive into it again, and the conductor, repeatedly stabbing the four points of a cross, looks fit to have a convulsion.

Ella turns to the side and whispers through nearly closed lips. "Walt," she says.

"What now?"

"When I fall over your lap, spill your Cracker Jacks and tell Mom I'm throwing up."

"Oh, cool. Good thinking, sister."

"We're not ever coming back here, are we?" Ella says.

"No way."

"We're being oppressed, and we want out," she says.

"Right on."

"These are the conditions necessary for—"

"Okay, okay."

The galaxy of violins bursts into freedom, abandonment, heaven. Buttressed on every note by second violins and violas and cellos, the first violins scream for liberation, sounding pretty good as a matter of fact, drunk with beat, injected with rhythm, as in-your-face as Michie Mee & L.A. Luv, as hip as Micheal Jackson's moonwalk, calling out to her and only her, and saying NOW Ella, do do do do DO DO DO DO do do do do DO IT NOW.

Ella collapses on her co-revolutionary, chest on his lap, arms splayed by his sides, head between his knees. She bugles as required and watches the battalion of Cracker Jacks cascade over her Lady Oxfords, overwhelm

Mother's kicking heels and salute the utterly still toes of the president of the women's church auxiliary. Ella listens to the sweet sound of her brother howling and allows herself to be lifted into strong arms. Never mind her sculpted hair and Sunday best, Mother is faster, stronger and more focused than most men. But she has also just been overthrown. Sayonara Massey Hall.

"Grab her coat, Walt," Mother whispers. "Hurry."

Doba
Dolly Reisman

"Red dilled tomatoes for breakfast?"

My grandfather's head hovered over the opening of a large glass pickling jar as he inhaled his favourite Russian delicacy. Dilled green tomatoes were normal, but red seemed to me to be eccentric. My family pickled everything, even watermelon. "It's for any time," my grandfather said, grunting with pleasure. Without pause to breathe, he fished out one more juicy red and popped it whole into his mouth. "Oy," he said, as he swallowed and smacked his lips together, "it's delicious."

Open jars full of fleshy red tomatoes were lined up on the kitchen table. Ropes of dill sat beside each jar soaking my mother's white embroidered table-cloth. A strong smell of garlic rolled off my grandfather. He swished around in the brine, squeezed a few tomatoes and triumphantly plucked one out.

"A beauty," he said. "It's perfect."

"Who is it for?" I asked.

Licking the juices running down his fingers, he looked up at me with a big smile and said, "Doba."

• • •

My great aunt Doba was arriving from Russia that afternoon. I had just turned sixteen a few months before, passed my driver's licence, straightened my hair and started wearing makeup. We were studying revolutionary Russia at school and had watched *Doctor Zhivago* in class. I attributed the love between Laura and Zhivago to the revolutionary furor of the times and desperately wanted to experience that kind of searing love. For a few weeks I espoused revolutionary and communist rhetoric at home. I talked about exploitation when my father talked about profits. My grandfather, who had abandoned most things Russian, dismissed my rants with, "Don't be crazy," or "You don't know what you're talking about."

In a family of capitalists, I was looking forward to having a communist comrade. In my reverie, I imagined my aunt stepping off the plane with Zhivago's child, a book of his poetry tucked under her arm. But in reality, Doba lived alone in Russia. For years she refused to immigrate to Canada, insisting that she couldn't leave the graves of her three sons to a future of vandalism and decay.

My grandfather sent her monthly packages: food bundled inside clothing, money sewn into the sleeves of old threadbare jackets, hidden in pockets and in the soles of worn-out shoes. He never knew if these packages would reach her given that the KGB scrutinized each piece of mail, but since Doba survived from package to package, my grandfather risked sending them out. When the regime finally loosened its reins on Jewish emigration, my grandfather sent her an invitation via first class post. The Russian officials acquiesced, and Doba agreed to live with her Canadian family in our house, in the basement bedroom that I sometimes used when my friends slept over.

• • •

My mother sent me to pick up pastries and cakes from Robert's Kosher Sephardic Bakery.

"Doba will be hungry," she said. "People starve in Russia."

I dressed carefully, wearing my favourite revolutionary outfit—long blue jeans fraying on the bottom and a black V-neck sweater underneath a Nehru-collared jacket, my unruly black hair pulled back into a ponytail. My style was more Mao than Stalin, but Doba wouldn't mind and I hoped that Joseph, the baker's son, would find me exotic.

Joseph was in the kitchen at the back of the store. He was humming to himself as he iced a multi-tiered wedding cake. He watched me as I entered the store, icing without looking. He winked at me and mouthed, "Good morning." My body began to burn.

Robert's Bakery was owned by the Serfaty family, Moroccan Jews. They spoke French and, although they weren't Orthodox, their baking was. Their non-dairy *parve* cakes were famous amongst the upwardly mobile Orthodox Jews for being as rich as any of those made from butter and cream.

"Mrs. Firestone's daughter," Mrs. Serfaty announced, catching me ogling her son. She smiled before hollering into the back, "Joseph! Get the order for Mrs. Firestone!" She looked me up and down with a mother's stern eye then added: "Her lovely daughter is here." I blushed.

Joseph emerged from the back room balancing a tower, one cake box stacked higher than the next. He'd arranged them in an illogical manner— not according to size but to whim, so that one box sat precariously on top of the other. Joseph had large Omar Sharif eyes, black hair and tanned skin. He smelled like fresh bread. He handed me the stack of cakes, but I was mesmerized with him beside me. Joseph laughed—his eyes twinkled with mischief as he took my hand and placed it on the top box then curled my fingers around the white string—the very string my grandfather would use to wrap around the bundles of clothing he sent to Russia.

A tingling swept up my arm and went directly to my heart. I gasped and couldn't grip the string or carry the boxes or even move. If I budged, I was sure I would drop the cakes and flatten them beyond recognition. A long line of young, humbly dressed Orthodox women—hair covered and jostling their infants—had formed and were waiting to be served. The women's impassive eyes staring at my immodest clothing and exposed head made me feel as if I were a disbeliever, a goy, and made me want to get out of there. I swung the cakes off the counter, smiled politely at Joseph, mumbled thank you and left.

"Good-bye, Mrs. Firestone's daughter," was the last thing I heard Joseph say as the door closed behind me.

• • •

When I returned home, there were six cars full of aunts and uncles and cousins crowding our circular driveway. I parked on the side of the road in front of our house. A stand of birch trees blocked my view, but I could hear my father and his two brothers arguing. Their voices were carried on the light breeze and soared above the trees.

I walked up the driveway.

"We should take the highway," my father said.

"But the traffic will be terrible, so we should stay off the highway," Uncle Frank said as he jiggled the change in his pocket.

"What do you know? The traffic is bad, but even still, the highway is always the fastest way there," said Uncle Sol, the middle brother. "We should do both. First, go around, then get on the highway later."

"Are you crazy?" yelled Uncle Frank, his voice tightening as it grew in volume.

"Who are you calling crazy?" asked Uncle Sol.

"Enough," said my father. "We're talking about a drive, not Hitler or Stalin."

"Yossi," my grandfather said. "Come."

"Okay Pa," my father answered. End of discussion. The leader had been chosen.

As we proceeded west on Highway 401, I turned around to see my uncles, aunts and cousins flailing their arms around. We were sufficiently far enough away from them that I couldn't hear them. But I knew they were screaming: "Where the hell are you going? It's the wrong way!" Oblivious to the commotion he had caused, my grandfather sat in the middle seat, focused on the road in front of him, with a gallon of red dills perched between his thighs. "Gold," he said. "Russian gold." He put a cigarette between his lips and let it dangle. "Doba," he said gently, "she'll like it."

• • •

We arrived at the airport an hour early, just in case. My grandfather stood in front of the frosted glass doors, straining to see each passenger as they exited after clearing customs.

"Pa," my father said. "Sit."

My grandfather silenced him with a stern look. He wanted to be standing when he met his past.

I paced back and forth in front of the doors waiting for my great aunt, but consumed by thoughts of Joseph. Pins and needles, I still buzzed. I shook the blood back into my hand, breathed deeply and tried to quiet my heart. My experience with men was limited to a failed relationship with a small-time petty pusher, short, cute and stupid. We had spent the entire summer in basements. My boyfriend and his friends would smoke up while I watched. My boyfriend didn't mind that I didn't smoke so long as I let him put his hands wherever he wanted. He'd get high and horny. He'd touch my breasts while kissing me and arch his groin into my leg. I would stay still as a statue, worried that he might want to go all the way. I had wondered how long he'd put up with kissing and dry humping. Weeks before Doba arrived, I walked around the house practising Russian. I begged my grandfather to teach me a few words. But he said that even if he could live forever, he would never go back to Russia and he would never again speak that language. I gave up begging him for new words and concentrated on saying "*da*" and "*nyet*" with the best Russian accent I could. One night when my boyfriend asked me to go all the way I said, "*Nyet.*" He said he didn't understand the language and that he didn't understand me, so he broke up with me on the spot. Joseph, I was sure, was more sophisticated. He had more promise. After all, he had a French accent.

When notice of Doba's plane landing blinked across the screen, the tribe of us gathered in one spot beside my grandfather. He pulled a small black and white photo of Doba as a young woman out of his pocket and compared that image with each and every passenger filing through the doors. No. No. No.

"Doba," my grandfather yelled. "Doba!" She stood at the entrance, hidden, despite the oppressive heat, by a black wool dress, holding her one small satchel. Fifty years had passed since the photo, but her face, now covered with wrinkles and lines and layers of flesh on her jaw line, was recognizable. An anxious look was frozen across her face. She looked like a child. Lost.

Doba searched the crowd, her eyes darting from one end of the hall to the other. After glossing over each family member, she squinted and then traced my grandfather's face with her eyes. Her lip quivered. Recognition. Tears spilled down her cheeks. My grandfather beckoned her over with a slight flourish of his hand. Doba stayed in her place, rigid with fear. My grandfather stepped over the roped-off boundary and marched toward her clutching his glass bottle. As he advanced, Doba retreated, until she was up against the glass barrier as if she were waiting for the guns, for the police, for someone to order her to move, for someone to shoot. My grandfather put down the jar and held his hands open. He softly called her name. He said a few things to her in Russian to put her at ease. Doba put down her satchel. My grandfather moved forward to embrace her. They had a quick and efficient hug.

Doba came from Russia with bad teeth. Some gold, some black and some missing. Doba barely spoke English. She opened her mouth wide and smiled broadly while nodding her head emphatically at everything that was said to her. "How was your flight, Doba? Are you hungry, Doba? Do you have to go to the bathroom, Doba?"

After the drive home, and after we ate coffee and cake around the kitchen table, I showed Doba to her new room. Like a little girl stalling for time, Doba dragged her hand over every surface as we made our way from the kitchen, through the large foyer, and down the stairs. Doba kept smiling and shaking her head back and forth in disbelief.

When we got to her room I said, "Doba, this is your room."

"Your r-r-r-r..." she tried.

"No," I said and took her hand and put it on her chest. "My room."

"My room," she repeated.

I introduced her to every part of the room. "My bed. My cushion. My floor. My drapes. My carpet. My lamp." Doba repeated each word slowly in her broken, accented English.

Doba pulled out a picture of a vibrant young woman with fierce, dark eyes and bangs that cut across a large square face. The woman stared defiantly at the camera—inconvenienced by having her picture taken. She had a savage beauty about her.

"Doba?" I asked, pointing at her.

"No," she said. And then very gently taking the photo out of my hand, she said, "Rifka. My," she placed her hand on her chest, "sister." Rifka was my grandmother. She died when I was two years old. Killed herself with an overdose of sleeping pills. It was my father who found her.

Doba placed the picture beside her bed. She showed me more pictures of her sons, handsome young boys with the same dark, intense family eyes. As I left her room she took my face in her hands and held it tight. She said a few things in Russian that I didn't understand, but I nodded as if I did. Then she stared into my face for a long time. I could see my grandmother's eyes, her son's eyes and my own eyes all reflected in hers.

• • •

The next night at dinner, I ate quickly.

"Sarah," my father said, "there is plenty. You don't have to eat so fast? What will Doba think of us? That we're barbarians?"

At the mention of her name, Doba smiled with a mouth full of food.

"I'm eating fast," I said, "so I can call Rochelle and finish up our project on revolutionary Russia." I lied.

My grandfather tsked at the mention of revolution and at the mention of Russia.

While the rest of my family lingered over a meal of borscht and stewed chicken, I called Joseph. Locked in my parents' bedroom, I stood beside the phone, looking at myself in the large mirror that covered an entire wall. My heart beat wildly as I waited for the first ring. In an attempt to calm myself, I focused on my reflection in the mirror. I noticed everything that was wrong with me. I looked young and unsophisticated. My hair was a mass of tangled curls and my eyes were too close together. At least Joseph couldn't see me.

One ring. I straightened my back.

Two rings. I adjusted my blouse, angling it to one side so the top of my shoulder was exposed. This was my idea of risqué.

I fluffed my hair, tossed it from my eyes.

Three rings.

"Robert's Bakery," a young man answered.

"Hello," I said.

"Hello."

His voice was gentle with a slight French accent.

"Hi," I said, again.

"Would you like to place an order?"

"An order?"

"Cakes. You want to order some?"

Silence.

"Would you like to place an order?"

For the third time I said, "Hello."

"Hello." He cleared his throat.

"Is this Robert's son?" And before he had a chance to answer I blurted out, "This is Mrs. Firestone's daughter."

There was a long pause. Then a sigh. Another pause. I could hear his rapid breathing and the chime of the bell that went off every time the store door opened.

"This is Robert's son," he said, slowly.

I could hardly breathe.

"Joseph," he added. His voice was smooth and calming and sent a thrill right through me, causing the hairs on my arms to stand straight up.

"Hello, Joseph," I said. "My name is Sarah."

There was another pause that felt like eternity.

"Ah, Sarah. So, you want to order some cakes?"

I hadn't thought this far ahead and didn't know what to say.

He continued. "You want to add to your mother's usual order?" And then he paused and I felt as if I was right beside him. I could imagine the curious look on his face as he talked to me. His voice betrayed a hint of puzzlement. A drop of uncertainty—he was on unfamiliar ground. "Or is this specially for you?"

I let out a tiny gasp and sat on the bed.

"Is it?" he pressed.

I could hear his mother in the background asking him to come. He covered the mouthpiece and mumbled something to her, but I couldn't make it out.

"Well," I said. The doorknob to my parents' room turned. I stood up.

"Yes," Joseph said. "What would you like?"

"I would like…" I swallowed. "I would like to have coffee with you." I blurted it out then held my breath and waited for him to respond.

"Joseph!" His mother called to him.

"One minute," he answered. And then to me: "Okay, I'll pick you up in an hour."

Joseph hung up without another word. I stood looking at the receiver, as if it had some unseen power. Then, coming to my senses, I slammed the receiver down and bolted out of the room. I'd have to get ready; *he* would be here in an hour!

∴

Downstairs, my grandfather had cornered Doba in his kitchen office, where he sat and read the Yiddish paper and answered the phone. He was holding his false teeth in his hands.

"See," he said showing her how well they worked, slipping them in and out of his mouth, practically hands free. "A perfect fit."

"No," said Doba. Her hands were clasped tightly over her mouth and she looked horrified. My grandfather began to bite into hard foods: apples and carrots, anything to prove the durability of his new bought-and-paid-for teeth. It was when he threatened to bite through a piece of wood that my father intervened.

"Pa," he said. "You're frightening her."

"Fright-en-ing," Doba repeated.

My grandfather moved towards the main floor powder room.

"Come," he said to Doba.

"No!" she said, defiantly.

"Don't be silly, Doba. Come. Look."

Doba sat down in her chair and refused to budge.

"Sarah, tell her to come and look," my grandfather pleaded.

"Zeyde," I said, "leave her alone." I was desperate to get ready for Joseph.

"Oy," he said, "you too."

My grandfather began to drag her chair out of the kitchen and into the hallway.

"Pa!" my father said.

"Don't mix into my business."

Doba held onto the bottom of the chair and screamed, "Oy, Oy, Oy!"

One cry built on the other, crescendoing in a mournful, gut-wrenching wail. I covered my ears to block out the sound. My father stood up, my grandfather waved him off.

"Stand up," my grandfather ordered Doba.

"Zeyde," I pleaded. "Stop. You're upsetting her."

He tried to drag her to her feet. Doba grabbed my hand and begged me to stay.

"Sarah, Sarah. Oy, oy, oy! "

When the doorbell rang we all jumped. I walked to the door with Doba attached; she wouldn't let go of my hand. I opened the door and invited Joseph inside.

My grandfather looked at Joseph and then shuffled off to the kitchen, giving Doba a reprieve. I introduced Joseph to my father and then to Doba. My father said a polite hello and Doba covered her mouth and bowed her head.

"I'll be home in an hour," I yelled as I peeled Doba's hand off mine and said, "I promise."

• • •

Joseph picked me up in the large white bakery van used to make cake deliveries. I let myself in the passenger's side and slid into the ripped leather seat. There were two seats in the front before a long cab full of white boxes for weddings, bar mitzvahs and brises: deliveries he'd have to make now. I realized that this was our date.

Joseph drove me around the city stopping at the various synagogues that had ordered his goods for their morning events. He explained that the recipes they used at the bakery were secrets handed down from his paternal grandmother, who used to supply the whole Sephardic community in Morocco with cakes. The recipes had passed down to his father, who was a master baker, to his mother and, finally, to him. His sisters had children to raise and no time for the bakery where Joseph headed every morning at four, to fire up the ovens for the day.

Joseph's descriptions of large vats of dark chocolate swirling into white cake mix made me hungry. After driving through every Orthodox section of the city, he took me back to his apartment. Joseph lived on the third floor of a six-floor walk-up. His apartment was empty except for a large mattress spread out in the middle of the living room. A map of Morocco, the country he had emigrated from, was pinned onto a large square corkboard attached to his wall.

Joseph stared at me, almost through me. "Mrs. Firestone's daughter," he said. "What would you like to order?" He laughed and began undoing his shirt. The sight of his naked skin caught me off guard. I backed away. "Come on," he said. "You have to want something." He moved forward. He flashed a big white-toothed smile at me. I thought of Doba's guarded smile, her lips protecting her decaying teeth from view.

"Could I have a glass of water?" I asked. My mouth was parched, my heart beating way too fast.

"Sure. If that's what you want to have, you can have it."

He put one hand on his belt and left it there as he backed into the kitchen, grabbed a glass with his other hand and flipped open the tap so it drained into the glass.

The glass hovered at crotch level.

I closed my eyes and tried to remember him in his bakery hat and white apron behind the bakery counter. I had often imagined myself leaping over the counter for Joseph. But here in his living room there was nothing between us.

"I want to go home," I said.

He sighed and unhooked his belt.

"Maybe you should just take me home," I said.

"Home?"

Joseph undid his belt buckle and the top button of his trousers.

"Yeah, back to my place."

He paused. Ran his hand through his cropped hair, his tongue worrying his mouth as he surveyed the room. I backed away towards the door. He snapped his head around, his eyes landing on my hand resting on the door latch.

"You don't have to go," he said.

"I do."

"I'll take you back, after."

He began to slowly unzip.

"I have to go back to Doba," I said. "She's all alone."

"She's fine," he said.

"She's scared. In fact terrified."

There was a long moment during which Joseph didn't move. He was going over his options. And I was going over mine. His eyes softened. He zipped up his pants, buttoned his shirt and drove me all the way home.

• • •

Doba was sitting in the kitchen, staring out the window, when Joseph dropped me off. It was morning, Russian time. It pained me to think that this was her morning ritual, looking out into nothingness—where were all her comrades when she needed them? Of course she was better off in Canada. Doba acknowledged me with a small nod and I went into the kitchen to see her.

"Doba. Comrade." I said. "*U tebja vsjov porjadke?* How are you?" Her face lightened and then immediately fell. She shrugged her shoulders and then they heaved. A torrent of tears fell onto the table beneath her, onto a picture of her three smiling boys. I picked the picture up and looked at my cousins. All of them dead.

• • •

A few weeks later, Doba arrived home with a swollen face. My grandfather had won. Doba smiled nervously, then winced in pain. In her hand she held a small package containing her teeth. Blood-drenched cotton gauze stuck to her gums.

"Does it hurt?" I asked.

"Hurt," she repeated.

"Ouch," I tried to explain.

"Ouch," she repeated.

"Hurt, ouch," I said, pointing to her mouth.

And finally she said, "Da. Hurt. Ouch." And then she began to wail, "Oy, oy, oy!"

The swelling went down after a few days, though the bruising took weeks to disappear. All Doba could eat were liquids or solid foods that had been blended into mush. Doba retreated to her basement bedroom. She refused to come and have her meals with us. I was the only one she talked to, the only one she'd agree to see. She slept during the day and sat by the kitchen window at night. Her English was rudimentary but she made no effort to learn new words. It didn't matter because she had descended into a state of silence. It was hard to tell if she wouldn't, or couldn't speak.

• • •

It was during this period of her solitude that Doba and I spent lots of time in her room getting to know one another. In truth we spent a lot of time doing nothing, but somehow this made me feel closer to her. We would sit in her dark room—Doba insisted that the drapes be closed—while she stared at a blank wall and I watched her. My mother assumed I was teaching her English, but Doba's interest in the language had waned. Sometimes I'd bring my homework downstairs and read about Marx, Lenin and Trotsky. I'd try to tell Doba about them and the importance of the revolution, at least the way I saw it, but just the mention of Stalin was enough to make her take out the picture of her sons and rock back and forth on the bed as she looked at them.

One day, in an attempt to lift her spirits and get her out of the house, I took Doba to school for show-and-tell. I felt sorry for her and hoped she'd enjoy meeting my friends. The title of my presentation was "Stalin and My Great Aunt." Doba dressed carefully that morning, wearing a long black skirt and a multi-coloured shirt with tassels hanging off the neckline. She pulled her hair back into a bun; a line of bobby pins on each side kept any wayward hairs in place. She proudly took my arm as we walked the half-mile to my school. There I was walking with a real-life Russian Matryoshka nesting doll. We walked past the ravine and up to Bathurst Street. When crossing the road, Doba held my hand. Janice and Rachel, who normally walked with me, raced ahead, all the while looking back in alarm. Doba and I promenaded through the curving streets in the rich, robust autumn light.

Doba stood at the front of the room while I talked about the hardships in her life and her escape from Russia. Of course she had no idea what I was talking about. Still, she eagerly spread out pictures of her husband and children for the class to see. At the end of my presentation the class applauded. Doba beamed and she broke into a huge, toothless grin. At the sight of her bare gums the class erupted into laughter. Doba quickly covered her mouth with her right hand while clutching the pictures of her family in her left.

After two weeks, Doba got her full set of false teeth. For the first few days she had a perpetual smile plastered on her face and it seemed that her sadness had ended. But after three days, the smile faded again.

Doba became withdrawn and depressed. Every day she wore the same black dress with a square collar bordered in a worn piece of fake velvet. Thick, opaque support stockings were rolled down to her ankles. I rarely went to her room anymore. I couldn't stand her sadness. She never smiled, and spent days weeping over the picture of her three young sons, all of them dead before the age I was now.

There were many discussions about her moving to a nursing home.

My parents were worried that in her depression she might hurt herself.

"She'll be safer at the home," they'd say.

"But will she be happier?"

I never got an answer.

A few weeks later, I got home from school, ran downstairs and found Doba packing. All of her possessions were crammed into one small suitcase, everything except her pictures of her children, which she had cut up into tiny little pieces and placed neatly at the side of her bed. My father and my grandfather were waiting upstairs to drive her to her new home. My father had used his connections and made arrangements for her. Doba marched solemnly up the stairs.

"Doba," I called.

She kept walking. Without protest. Without a sound. Without turning back.

• • •

Home from school on the cold bleak February day one month after Doba was sent away, I found my grandfather sitting alone in the kitchen, an unopened jar of red dill tomatoes beside him.

"Zeyde," I said, "what's wrong?"

For a long while my grandfather didn't answer. The dull grey light was turning to darkness.

"Zeyde!"

My grandfather fumbled with his wire-rimmed reading glasses. He unhooked them one ear at a time.

"*Toit,*" he said. Dead.

"Doba?" I asked.

He nodded, then motioned to the jar of tomatoes. She had never even opened them. She had never eaten the tomatoes or lived any kind of life, or seen her children grow or grandchildren be born. My grandfather blotted his eyes with his hanky. I sank into a kitchen chair and swallowed my rage and tears.

• • •

That night my family gathered at our house, but I didn't want to see them. I wanted to find Joseph; to be with Joseph. I waited in the alley in back of the bakery for him to close up. It was bitterly cold but I felt nothing. He turned the key one last time and tested the large steel door to be sure it was locked. I came up quietly behind him. He shuddered when I put one hand against his back and one over his mouth. He struggled to turn around, but relaxed when he saw me. He smiled, smiled as if sweetness were in his blood. His eyes were soft and inviting and so full of hope. I craved him. Craved his hope, and clung to him as he pinned me up against the side of the van and kissed me. My heart exploded. He unlatched the cargo door. He kissed my eyelids. He swept aside the cakes and trays to be delivered for morning prayers, and fell on top of me. Doba was dead. He licked my lips and gently parted them. Doba's lips were cold. He kissed my face all over. Doba was going to be buried in the ground. He travelled down my body. There were so many things I wanted to ask Doba. How many sleeping pills did you take, Doba? Did dying hurt, Doba? He finger-hooked my panties and slid them down. Are you with your children now, Doba? Are you happy now, Doba? Did Stalin kill your whole family, Doba? And then bursting out of my mouth, "Oy, oy, oy. Oy, oy, oy."

My Father's South-Asian Canadian Dictionary

Priscila Uppal

includes the names of Canadian prime ministers and MPPs.
(We are from a government town, a government attitude on ice.)

I know what it means to lodge a complaint, submit a form,
participate in the census, just as I know that *being Canadian*

is the greatest pride on earth. My poetry comes out of
my father's chest, tough and wholehearted, half-paralyzed

but brave. We believe in *pronunciation, adjudication* and
all for the nation. We believe in *universal health care,*

teddy bears and all-you-can-eat buffets. In my father's
knuckles are the bare bones of a family he practically invented.

What does it mean to be an *Uppal*? It means *diligence,*
excellence. It means *humility* and *finding your own ways*

in and out. Before me, it meant *business school, medicine,*
looking carefully and effectively at all financial options.

It meant *buying insurance* and *thinking about the future,*
and *marrying into a stable family with moral values.*

Institutional language is ours: *hypotheses, liabilities,*
rent or lease. Yet, hockey too: *boarding, hooking,*

right wing, top of the cage. I know little Punjabi, and we
always eat far more chicken à la king than curry, and

cheer loud for Queen Elizabeth and the Pope, but
my brother and I can both mimic a South-Asian accent

when we say: *Mahatma Ghandi, River Gange* or
You are such a smarty pants. In my father's eyes, we

are *ragamuffins, gallivanting around the neighbourhood,*
while others are *clowns,* or *con-men, with sweetheart deals.*

And when we come home to visit, he says, *please* and
thank you. And when he's lying scared in hospital beds

we say *our dad, a quadriplegic,* who knows what it
means to be *alive,* fellow citizens, more than anyone.

Recipes for
Dirty Laundry
Priscila Uppal

ANIMAL STAINS:
Apply vinegar and baking soda; then scrub.

Rosa knows Teresa is the pretty one: she has more problems. Today it's the bath. Water running, Rosa knows Teresa will be pouring in some of the red bubble bath that smells like raspberries her sister always finds enough money for when it's on sale. Sometimes Rosa uses it too, waiting patiently until all the bubbles disappear before calling for someone to take her out. Then, after Mamma or Teresa help her into a nightdress, she keeps the towel beside her, inhaling the faint scent of the berries on the cloth. Rosa only bathes on Sundays, but Teresa bathes whenever she wants.

Today the bath is a problem, Rosa can tell. Her bedroom is beside the bathroom so it's easier for her to go in the middle of the night. She can hold on to the walls until she reaches the Virgin Mary in a light blue and white frock, eyes and hands pointing to the heavens in prayer. It is a good picture, and Rosa, in the dark of the night, always knows which door is the right one. Today, lying down on her single bed, she can hear a faint sobbing from the Virgin Mary's direction like the hum from her old radio. She decides to get up, pushing against the guardrail for leverage.

Rosa slides her leg over the end of the bed where the guardrail doesn't intrude and puts on her brace, attaching the straps across her calves, slipping her fingers through the steel wires. She can tell where the straps should be from the marks over and under her knees, slightly darker than the rest of her skin, pressed like pleats in linen. She tries to be quiet. She doesn't want

Mamma to catch her taking a peak at her sister, which she likes to do when Teresa bathes. If the door is locked, she returns to her own bed, wraps her wool blanket around her shoulders and looks through one of her picture books, her favourite about a small girl in a red dress who meets a wolf in the forest. Resting the book across her chest, she imagines herself skipping off down a path in a forest to the washroom where Teresa is and, pushing her fingers in front of her nose, imagines the smell of bubble bath or leg cream, all flowery and sweet. Then sometimes Rosa pretends to shave her legs, the way she has seen Teresa do it, propping her ankle on the bed board instead of the edge of the tub and scraping against her skin with a hairbrush. She even moans quietly, the way Teresa does once in a while, splashing the water just over her skin, hands hidden and eyes closed, cheeks flushed and breathing heavily, a sound like the soft and quick bursts made when trying to open a stuck can lid.

Rosa has to use both of her hands to keep her leg straight when she drops it lightly on the carpet to head to the washroom. She can already imagine the back of Teresa's head, her long hair like roots descending into the water, and her long naked body half-covered in bubbles. If Mamma were to come down the hallway, collecting laundry from the hampers placed just outside of each door, it would be easy to pretend she's just checking to see if she can use the bathroom. She could even hold on to the elastic waistband of her pants and wriggle her upper body a little.

Today the door is locked. Rosa frowns, but then remembers. She has an excuse to go in. Teresa is crying: she has a problem. Rosa might be able to help. She knocks. No sound, not even sobbing. Resting her head against the door, Rosa's cheeks flatten into the Virgin Mary's tight hands.

"Get away from the door, Rosa."

Rosa doesn't budge. "But you're crying. I can help."

"Rosa, listen to me. I'm fine. Just get away from the door." Teresa's voice is firm, but low.

"You feel sad, Tera?" Rosa wishes she could get on the floor and peak through the crack, but she wouldn't be able to get up without help.

"Go away Rosa. Right now!" Rosa recognizes the "I don't have time for you" voice. Teresa doesn't use it often, but when she does, Rosa is expected to obey. As she bows her head beneath the Virgin Mary's chin, her eyes begin to tear.

"Sorry, Tera. I don't mean it."

Rosa hears sniffling. "Just go and read and maybe I'll tuck you in later." Then guitars and drums, insistent and hard, blare through the door. Rosa's voice can't compete, so she ambles back to her room.

After taking off her brace and placing it neatly upright, Rosa crawls back into bed. She likes to lie down all alone, pretend she's wearing white shoes and a red dress with fancy beads, and that there's a bouquet of pink flowers by the nightstand given to her by some boy. Tonight she pretends this boy has a ticket to the school dance. Last month Teresa took her. Rosa liked handing over the ticket. "I'm here," it said to her. "Look at me." Some boys were turned away, ones with tickets too, who smelled and walked funny. But they never turned Rosa away. Miss Brown told her she looked pretty, and Teresa bought her an orange drink at the booth, leaving Rosa with her. Rosa didn't need to go with a boy, that's just what a lot of girls did. Teresa danced with boys, close if the songs were slow, like the songs she usually liked to listen to in the bath. Before, dances had been a problem, when Teresa and Rosa were at separate schools. But now Rosa also attends the high school, though she stays in the same class, not like Teresa who spends her day moving from one room to another with different textbooks. Teresa doesn't have class with Miss Brown, but Rosa does. Miss Brown helps Rosa with her sewing, since she is one of the few allowed to sew.

"That girl's gonna get in trouble, Mamma. I had a dream—" Papa's voice is harsh and he coughs when he yells too loud. Mamma must be rubbing his back, Rosa thinks. Maybe she could check, make sure Papa hasn't hurt his chest, but Mamma doesn't like it when she knocks on Papa's door without asking. "You need to be sure of his mood," Mamma told her. "He's sick."

"I'm sick too," Rosa replied.

"No, you're not, Rosa. Don't say that again. And don't say that to the neighbours. They don't understand."

Rosa can hear Mamma stomping down the hallway. She is crying too, and Rosa imagines a white handkerchief dangling from her fingers, grey hair hanging out the back of her net.

"Teresa. Get out of there right now!" Mamma knocks vigorously. Rosa lifts her back off the bed to get a look into the hallway. This is certainly "a commotion," what Mamma said Rosa shouldn't do outside in front of anyone, that if someone speaks to her she should pretend she can't speak English and point to the house. Maybe Mamma can't help making "a commotion"; Rosa sometimes couldn't help it. Maybe Mamma thinks the bathroom is dirty or the music is too loud.

"Just a minute, Mamma."

"Right now!"

The music stops. Hands clenched into fists, Mamma turns and thumps down the stairs. Rosa can hear the plug being pulled, the water swirling and burping down the drain, and Teresa getting out of the tub. Soon after,

the lock unfastened, Teresa emerges in a white terry-cloth robe, black hair
frizzed up even though it is wet and should be straight and heavy. Teresa
didn't comb it, Rosa thinks. But she always gave her hair a good combing
in the bath or else it hurt the next day and Mamma would need to help her,
the way Mamma always combs Rosa's hair.

"Teresa Maria Campanous!"

"One minute, Mamma! I have to get some clothes on!"

"Ha! Clothes! You better put some clothes on and keep them on—"

"Mamma, I'm coming! Please!"

"If I could walk..." The coughing stops Papa's sentence.

Teresa halts at Rosa's door, her face red and prunish. "You go to sleep, Rosa."

Rosa nods and pulls the covers over her head, imaging herself in a car
with guitar and drum music playing, wind from an open window sweeping
up her hair. After fifteen minutes, Rosa wants to close her door, but doesn't
want to get up. She hates it when people talk loud, but not loud enough to
pass through doors. Then it's just noise and it hurts to concentrate.

A half-hour later, her sister walks by again. "Tera," she whispers, but Teresa
turns off the light off in the bathroom and shuffles to her room at the other
end of the hall.

Once again, Rosa puts on her brace and steps quietly out her door. She
holds onto the walls, past the bathroom, past Papa's room, to Teresa's room.
Without knocking, she inches the door open with her foot and Teresa,
crouched on the floor, shoves some clothes under the bed. Looking up,
Teresa sighs, but with a finger against her lips waves to Rosa to come in and
quietly shut the door.

"You need those washed, Tera?"

Teresa wipes her eyes and kicks a pant leg further underneath the bed.
"No."

"I can wash them."

"No, Rosa. And don't tell Mamma." Teresa has slipped back into her bath-
robe. Rosa notices how red her legs are and that the yellow sponge from the
bathroom in her hand has red blotches on it.

"You cut yourself shaving? You gonna take another bath?"

Teresa doesn't answer. She gets up, sits on the edge of her bed, and pats
the place beside her. Rosa sits down. Rosa likes Teresa's comforter. It's pink,
like the walls.

"Pretty clothes, Tera. Can I have them, if you're gonna throw them away?"
Rosa likes to get clothes from Teresa. Teresa has store-bought clothes instead
of wearing only the dresses Mamma makes.

"No. They're no good. They're garbage."

Rosa gasps, knowing Mamma does not like it when they throw things in the trash.

"Good for rags then, Tera. Good for—"

"Listen, Rosa. This is important," Teresa stresses, gripping Rosa's arm. "And you don't tell Mamma."

"OK."

Rosa concentrates, staring at the pink comforter. There are things Rosa must not tell Mamma. That's what sisters do, she knows, keep secrets. Rosa waits, but Teresa's hand starts shaking, and the sash on the white robe grows a spot of pink.

"Oh, Christ." Teresa pulls off the white robe in front of Rosa, her slim naked body with small, tight breasts and just a triangle of hair between the legs open to Rosa's eyes, presses the sponge against her thighs, then grabs a large T-shirt from the back of the closet.

"Don't say that. You're not allowed to say that. Did Mamma do that to you?"

"No." Pulling the t-shirt over her head, the hem under her thighs, she sits back on the bed, takes her pillow and lays it over her lap. "An animal did," she adds, as if to her legs and not to Rosa. Now Rosa starts to shake, imagining the wolf from her picture book, his fangs bared and growling.

"Rosa, some boys are bad. This is our secret."

"Not the boys you dance with."

Teresa makes a noise like biting on hard candy. "No, not the boys I dance with, but that's only where the people are, the teachers." Rosa nods, holds out her hand to touch Teresa's legs.

"Don't touch, it hurts. Listen to me, Rosa. This is a secret." Rosa really must concentrate. The pink comforter is no help. She bites down on her lip, tasting her own blood, hot and salty.

"Some boys don't listen when you're alone with them. Don't be alone with a boy."

"You have problems because you're pretty," Rosa says, touching her tongue, blotting at the blood with her finger. She and her sister both have dark eyes and hair, but Rosa's is cut short since she can't brush the tangles by herself. Rosa's face is defined by the same long eyebrows and oval face, yet it's stretched wide, making all her features larger than Teresa's. Rosa has larger breasts and thighs too, a version of what Teresa might look like one day in middle age. Only the one leg has never grown into the shape of a woman.

"Oh Rosa, what did you do? Did you bite your tongue? Who told you that?" Teresa frowns, stroking the top of Rosa's head, blotting at her lip with the sponge.

"I heard Mamma and Papa say it about you. You get problems when you have a pretty girl in a big city. I'm not pretty like you. No problems for me."

"Rosa, a boy might ask you to go alone with them sometime. You don't go. You understand?"

Rosa taps her foot. She can't imagine any boy asking her to go away with him, although there had been the boy who offered to walk her to the washroom at the dance. Miss Brown said he was a nice boy, and he was. He smelled like pinecones, and he took her to the bathroom upstairs, the far one, he said, because Rosa must like to have fun. Rosa giggled, said she did, and he put his hand on her blouse to fix her button. Rosa laughed, because he missed her button. Then the door opened, a young girl came out drying her hands against her yellow dress, and so she went in after and then he took her back to the dance. He hadn't asked her to go away with him. He hadn't asked her anything, not even her name. One day, Rosa knows, Teresa will go away. Go away with a boy, marry and have babies like their mamma.

"It's hot there, Tera?" Teresa nods.

"I know," Rosa says, taking the tube of cream off Teresa's end table, "I'll put this on your legs and you'll feel better."

Rosa opens the bottle and squeezes the white liquid into a mound onto Teresa's sponge. Teresa stretches out her legs, and Rosa smells the flowers, but another smell too, something Rosa can't make out, a strong smell, not very nice, maybe the smell of an animal, like her sister said, like the smell on your clothes when dogs get too close to you. Then she remembered walking one day with Teresa when a dog peed on the fence next door. Rosa laughed at the funny streak it made, and Teresa told her dogs do that to show where they've been. Now Rosa, too many images in her mind, is confused. Berries. Wolf. Boys. Trash. Dogs. She can't imagine everything together. Better to concentrate on Teresa's legs.

"You smell nice, Tera," Rosa tells her, but Teresa isn't looking at her. Her face is covered with her arm and she curls herself up into a ball.

When Rosa goes back to bed, instead of looking at her picture book, she takes out her hairbrush and pretends to shave her legs until the bristles scratch her skin. "Look at me. I'm here," she says to the wolf and the girl in the red dress. Then she turns off the light, and thinks about her secrets.

TEAR STAINS:
You're the only one who notices them.

The week before Magdala married, all those years ago in Portugal, her mamma passed down her wedding dress and her mourning dress. Her own husband had been dead almost twelve years so she didn't need to wear the full black suit with the veil. She only needed to wear black. Magdala had been staring at the white frilly fabric, the delicately beaded cuffs and collar, wondering if the women had already altered the waist and the lace on her shoulders to suit her own figure, when the black attire was thrown on top of her already full arms: an ankle-length starched skirt, a long, billowy, black knit blouse and a short veil. "Every woman needs to prepare, Magda," her mamma told her. "My mamma did the same for me. She wore both of those. You're next." She hugged her daughter in rapture, the dresses collecting under Magdala's chin and bristling her ears, the black veil crossing her face like a net. She could barely see her mamma hunched over, arms wound tightly as string, pinching her ribs. As the smell of the bread rising in the kitchen mixed with the sting of the boiled onions and zucchini, mother and daughter thought of all the preparations that still had to get done before morning. Suddenly, they both started to cry.

Now Magdala sheds her tears on paper, the letters she receives from back home. News about the others, cousins she's never met, and her only sister, Maria, who stays home with her mamma. They try to keep in touch, offer news about the weather, gardens, weddings or births, and Magdala smells each sheet of paper as it passes behind the next one as if Portugal were contained in the neat lines and could be unzipped like a package. Then she carefully folds the papers, ties them with string, and adds them to the others neatly stored in the shoebox of her closet. She received another letter today, but won't read it until all the laundry is hung and she can retreat to the basement with a cup of hot tea.

As Magdala clips another white undershirt to the line, she wonders, not for the first time, why they decided on this house over twenty years ago. There were other houses made of red brick on the same street, but they were red, not grey, and this house's driveway was clearly marked by two stone walls on each side of the entrance, two stone lions carved at the feet of the road. She wanted the house because of the privacy, the black gates around the front and back and those grey walls. Now she wishes she had chosen one of the houses with a shared driveway or an open front yard where the children could have played ball or skip and not run into gate or stone. But there was the issue of money. That's why they'd picked the Italian neighbour-hood in Toronto instead of the Portuguese one. It was closer to Tonio's work and they didn't have a car. She thought it wouldn't matter since they were sending the children to English schools and teaching them bits of Portuguese around the house. But now Teresa knows more Italian than Portuguese, picked up from years of talking to other children and their parents on the street, and Rosa, well Rosa, when they realized what was wrong with her, they were thankful she would grow up in a neighbourhood where the children might tease her in a language she wouldn't understand. But Rosa too learned Italian. It was only Magdala who did not, and when she hangs her laundry, which is almost always since Tonio's undershirts and sheets need cleaning on a daily basis, she can barely see the neighbours let alone speak to them. Shaking out a wet sheet, Magdala tries to remember the last time she spoke a word outside the house or the grocery store, when she didn't just wave curiously over walls. Was it last summer? Last fall? Yes, it was last fall, when the Korean couple who run the corner store were robbed. A teenager in a ski mask hit the man over the head and asked for all the money. They called the police, Teresa told Magdala, but nothing could really be done about it, except that the Korean man had four stitches on his scalp. The next time Magdala went to buy a carton of milk, she'd said, "Sorry. So sorry to you and your wife." She felt like she was about to cry, and he looked confused, asked her if she needed help with something. "No. No. It's just good that you're in the neighbourhood," she said, but she knew she'd said everything wrong, should have made herself clear that she'd heard about the robbery. Stunned to be talking to someone, Magdala could barely get her change back in her purse and walk herself home.

There was another Portuguese family that lived down the street beside the parkette, but they moved. They had an extra large garden and even grew pumpkins in the fall. For a while, Magdala and the other woman exchanged vegetables, recipes and sympathy cards, although they never went for walks or had tea unless there was a chore involved. Children and husbands had to come first. But it was nice to buy bread or compare fabric prices together, to speak the language of her mamma and her sister with someone besides Tonio. Then, ten years ago, when the last of the woman's children had left home, she and her husband moved to North York, and Magdala was alone once again.

Magdala misses her mother, although she would never write that in a letter. It's alright for her mother to say she misses her, and Magdala is sure the letter in her pocket will contain this declaration, but for Magdala to say she misses her mother means there is trouble in her marriage, and trouble in the marriage is never something to share with one's mother. These kinds of things are not to be discussed. Her mamma had outlived her husband already by a generation, and Magdala couldn't help wondering what her mamma thought about her own life, her own marriage, if she had planned to be with Papa forever instead of her daughter and was deeply pained, or if she was secretly relieved that Papa had died quickly and young, that she would never have to see him suffer or lose interest in her. These are things Magdala cries over, because it isn't right to ask. And it isn't right either to ask why Mamma had been so intent for Magdala to marry an older man, her senior by twenty years. But she knows why. Their village was dying. All the young men were moving to cities, to other countries to find work. Tonio had money, was kind and was travelling to a better place, if a snowy one.

Oh, the snow! Magdala knows it's on its way. She can smell its crisp foreboding in the air. Only a few more weeks, maybe less, and she will no longer be able to hang her laundry outside, but will have to retreat into the basement to avoid all the falling leaves and frosts. Mamma, she thinks, staring up at all the billowing fabrics, how I wish I had stayed with Mamma, lain in her arms a little longer, not taken away her dresses whether she wanted to get rid of them or not. Soon Magdala will need the black dress. Tonio can't hold out much longer, it's only her constant care that has kept him alive for so long. The blood on the handkerchiefs spells his end, just as the first leaves on the ground spell the end of summer. The doctors are all pessimistic about his chances. Yet he holds on lazily, and her hands bleach out the secret messages she can't write to her mother, can't tell her neighbours.

What happened to that Italian boy who used to work on the cars at all hours of the night? Magdala doesn't know, and she can't ask. Teresa had liked him, and Magdala had worried maybe they were sweet on each other. Too young. Too young. My little Teresa must stay little forever, free of men, free of marriage, free of sickness and death, she thought then. Now she sees a daughter full of life, full of prettiness, full of thoughts Magdala never had. What was it she said? She wanted to take courses in business? Maybe open a clothing store in the west end before the rents rise too high? Yes, that was it, but Magdala had stopped listening, imagining a boy in a ski mask hitting her over the head to get her money. "Better to get married," she told her. "Have someone buy you a house, make a vegetable garden." Even that Italian boy would be alright, she thought, since he knows a trade. And Teresa listened, or else she got herself into trouble first and listened later, but now there is a ring, she showed her the ring, and that other boy in the car was the man's cousin, yes, and she'd been dizzy because she'd fallen on the sidewalk, which is why he took her home. There was no need to get so upset and Papa wouldn't stop about his dreams, but everything is fine. He's Portuguese too, but from Brazil. "Nice eyes, strong face and hands," Magdala told her daughter after shaking his hand for the first time. "A little dark, but that happens in Brazil. Everyone is mixed." Sheepishly, head bowed, Teresa said, "I will have to learn how to run a restaurant. He owns a restaurant, Mamma, with his brother. Maybe one day Rosa can help out, and we can open a clothing store, too." Magdala nodded happily, but wondered how much of it all was true. In the old days, Tonio would have gone out in the streets, asked around, met all the cousins and the rest of the family, but now Magdala just has to trust her daughter.

Once a year, Magdala bleaches the wedding dress to keep it fresh and white, make sure moths and mould don't have their way. Tough fabric, it has held for three generations and likely more if Teresa is careful when she has a daughter of her own. The long and simple skirt, straight cut with a thick circular line and laced at the waist, is probably back in style. The high neck and round pearl beads along the chest are elegant without being grand, the lace sash and cuffs symmetrical as butterfly wings. Wedding dress first, mourning dress afterwards. Magdala is lucky, the first in three generations who hasn't lost her husband a decade before the first child reached adulthood. And Rosa will be here to take care of her when she starts to slip. Just like her own sister and their mamma. Family tradition if one of the children is born that way. A curse on the child, but a blessing on the mother since she will never be left alone. And Magdala needs the help. Her back is already sore after only two loads of laundry. There are still cucumbers and zucchini to peel, and she promised to teach Rosa cross-stitches this afternoon. The house will need to be changed to suit her, Magdala reminds herself as the wooden pins clip each thought to the clothes and sheets. Shelves must be heightened, the garden properly marked, the bathroom cupboards switched and, of course, all the bedrooms must be rearranged so Rosa can start to learn to take care of Magdala. It won't be long after papa that she too…She will need to teach Rosa. Teach her things like what Magdala knows from the letters…

…the weather's hot. Mamma screams in her sleep. I worry. She's old. She talks about Papa. She never used to. She talks about her wedding and all the trips they were going to take before he died. Hated her own mamma for not telling her about boys and she was so scared when her belly started to grow. She drinks three jugs of water a day and walks back and forth to the bathroom all night…

A wall of white in front of her, blocking everything else from view, Magdala thinks of her wedding night in Portugal, how the town had danced under the yellow lanterns her family had hung from the trees, and Tonio, a few grey hairs across his temples, had twirled her in his arms, called her his little girl. Leaning against the stone bricks, another letter in her pocket, another load of laundry hung, she wonders who will send sympathy cards, and how they'll afford Teresa's wedding.

WINE STAINS:
Pour lots of salt onto the stain, dunk into cold water and rub out.

Inside Tonio are two dreams: fire and water. His wife, Magdala, helps lift his large back away from the bed, holds him across the armpits to prop up his pillow, then slowly releases him. He recovers like a blade of grass. Looking out the window, he can see his undershirts and sheets on the line in the back-yard, wooden pins marking the days he has survived in the trenches, all flags of white. "I surrender," he wants to tell his dreams. "I surrender." But still the shirts and sheets are hung.

Morning is roll call. Magdala peels off his shirt, throws it in her plastic basket. Then she pulls down the blankets, exposing limp legs like useless, splintered crutches, his olive skin wan and yellow without sun. She pats his thighs, meaning he should attempt to rise a little so she can slip off his underwear flipping it quickly inside out and back again to examine it for stains. Into the same basket they go, whether or not there are any. A washed pair then appears, white cotton with an elastic waistband, a thin stripe of blue or black across the top. He doesn't watch, can't look down there without shaking. The only time he mentions it is if the band has caught on any hair.

This morning Tonio was dreaming before the sun hit his face. Shielding his eyes, he still saw Magdala opening the door, already dressed and working. "Papa," she said. "Time to get up." The sun denies him of his dreams, though he's been trying to embrace them, keep himself in the dream's arms so it will end. He wants to know how everything turns out, what happens after the fire and water rush over him. Magdala inspects the sheets for stains, tucking in stray sides as she does so, and leans in as she kisses him on the forehead to smell for sweat. This morning she doesn't need to change the sheets. Maybe later. She checks three times a day, more if he screams.

There are bombs inside Tonio's body: little bombs that go off randomly but persistently in twos or threes. Hot, hot, hot they shoot up his arms and down his legs like burns, smelling like sulphur, stinging his nostrils. Tonio feels like he's had his hand on a hot stove for the last six years. And then there are the tides. Ones that swell inside his throat and want to rush out onto the bed, others that stir and churn inside his stomach as if a drain were plugged. They steam inside him, pound against his veins, pour out of his body. Every entry a spout. "Move on," he tells the tides. "Keep marching and you'll over-take them." Tonio knows the tides and the bombs are a part of him, and yet they are also enemies, trying to silence him, making it difficult for him to speak his words or tell his dreams. They don't want to be detected. Masters of camouflage.

"There are bombs, Magda." He wants to tell her more, but the small dish is in front of him and Magdala has put a plastic spoon in his right hand.

"The war is over, Tony. You're at home." She walks over to the window on the left side of his bed and opens the blinds. The sun rushes against her face, turning her into an outline. Tonio would rather the blinds were shut. It's harder to fall asleep in the afternoons with the sun in his face and his eyes are too sore to read any more. Because the blinds are cracked, even when shut the few missing rungs allow for light and the sight of his laundry waving in the breeze, his empty shirt sleeves helpless.

Tonio slams his hand down on the bed, trying to pound out his words. He starts to cough and Magdala rubs his back, procures a handkerchief and holds it in front of his mouth to catch the spit. "The doctor is coming tomorrow, Papa." He shakes his head and coughs harder. Magdala rests her basket, sighing as her body relieves itself of the burden of the weight, and calmly waits for the fit to pass. Sometimes she hums, trying to soothe him or, if his eyes are open, smiles to show him she's not worried. He tries to focus on the photographs hung on the right wall, pictures of the girls and Magdala when she was younger, recently arrived in Toronto, in front of the new house. Tonio, with hand gestures and broken English, had asked one of the neighbours, now he can't remember which, to take the photograph for them. The camera was also new. It was a time of new things. Rosa would be born in less than a year. Teresa three years later.

"No more doc—" Two bombs explode up Tonio's arms. His head slams against Magdala. She holds her face, biting her lip to hold in the pain. "Okay, Tony," she says. "No more doctors. It's easier on the children."

Tonio's fire abates and he hands her back the damp handkerchief. She throws it in the basket, places a white one on the nightstand. He feels small in the room, in the king-sized bed, as if he's been shrinking. He remembers when he was first brought in here, for good, he was sure the room didn't have enough air, that he wouldn't be able to get used to the cramped space. But, over the years, the room has become a whole land, a settler's field he has lost the strength to plough, and he anticipates that soon he will be reaped, shucked into a wooden barrel and delivered elsewhere. He starts to eat, the hot porridge massaging his gums. Magdala leaves the room, closing the door behind her.

One day Tonio might like to sleep with the window open, maybe dream about wind, but he can't reach. The one time he tried, Magdala caught him, screamed, and he lost his balance and fell on the floor. It took both girls to lift him back on the bed. "Don't move, Papa. You could hurt yourself," they warned him. He asked, "What do I do if there's a fire?" "There's no fire, Papa," they said. He tried to tell them, waving his fingers frantically through the air in circles like smoke. "Hold his hands down," Magdala told the girls. "He might hit himself." And they obeyed, strapping him down on the bed, unaware of his melting skin.

Tonio can hear the rumble of the washing machine through the vents, its starts and stops, the regular burbling of the wash cycle. He imagines his clothes, their stains, drowning in the water, spitting out into the basin. Before, they had talked about moving him to the basement. Fewer stairs, and Magdala spent most of her day down there doing chores. They could be closer. She could reach him earlier if needed. And he would have a window at ground level to call her when she was outside. "We could make it nice, Tony. I could hire someone to move all the furniture and put down a carpet." He protested. "Too much work for you, Mamma. You have enough to do already." But there were days he wished he would wake up and find himself down there in the basement, listening to the washing machine, dreaming of thunder and hot rains and bleached white sheets spinning.

In many of his dreams, Tonio is crawling in the garden, pushing down the lines of wooden stakes with his arthritic hands, his feet dragging behind in the dirt like heavy luggage. He can hear the push of the water and smell the pull of the smoke; this is when the dreams combine. To his left are all the fabrics hung on the line, motionless without wind, necklines drooped like people in prayer. The endless days he struggles in and out of those lines stand erect. "I surrender," he tries to say, but can't get the words out; he tries, but has to keep his mouth shut against the smoke, his eyebrows starting to burn. He can feel each individual hair parting. The neighbours, the ones he remembers from years ago, the Italian couple with the large van and the three boys, yes, it was the man who had taken the photograph for them the day they moved in, are in their backyard, drinking or walking, the boys playing ball or running under a sprinkler, yelling in English mixed with Italian. He can barely understand either, but he knows basic words. "Water," he yells, but no one hears him. They are busy playing and talking, and no one sees him crawling on the ground. The last time he had the dream, he got further and started to dig in the garden with his hands, pulling up cold, black soil. Maybe if he planted himself upside down and perfectly straight, like a carrot, he thought, it would all be over. He would have figured it out. He had been digging, holding his breath to keep out the elements, when the sun peeled open his eyes this morning.

Magdala returns with a letter, places it on his nightstand beside the handkerchief, smiling, her cheeks cracked with deep lines. "A letter, Papa, from Portugal. I'll read it to you later." Tonio nods, pleased to see her smiling, the ribbons of white hair twirled into a bun, reminding him of the flowers she wore on their wedding day.

"You're such a good woman, Magda." She pauses to scan his face, then kisses his forehead. Tonio feels sealed by her lips, to be opened later when she has the time to sit and love him. He knows she skips parts of the letters, probably when they ask about his health. He can tell. She pretends she can't make out the handwriting, that, out of practice, it takes her longer each time to make out the Portuguese, and then she flips the page behind the envelope. Sometimes she says, "Oh, this part isn't interesting to you. It's just a recipe." Sometimes she says nothing and hides her eyes.

"You should send your recipe for stains," he tells her, nodding his head vigorously as he usually does when he praises her. "They always come out." When the laundry comes back, he is often amazed by the clean slate in front of him, tells himself today, today, there will be no need for anymore. Today they will stay white...

Tonio wakes again to Magdala's voice rolling across her tongue and teeth like waves in their old speech, the letter held up in front of her reading glasses. "...the weather's hot...Mamma...drinks three jugs of water a day and goes back and forth to the washroom all night...Isn't that funny, Tony?"

He nods, gives her a little chuckle and sips the glass of wine she brought him, content she let him have some in the afternoon to help him sleep. He tries to make it last, hoping if he takes his time it won't flood his body, but already he can feel his toes filling up with fluid. He wants to tell his wife about the water dreams, how the water spreads over him like a thick wet blanket and he sinks. Wants to tell her how it feels not to breathe anymore. He wonders what her mamma dreams of, if she tells her daughter, if that is the part she skipped over in the letter. Tonio has never met anyone underneath the water in his dreams before, but maybe he hasn't been looking. Maybe they could meet, touch hands, get out of the dream together.

"What a big garden they have again back home," Magdala says, eyeglasses on her lap, face turned towards the window.

"You make the best zucchini."

"It was a good year, Papa," she sighs. "They grew big and firm. Maybe this year will be a good year, too."

"You did it Magda." Tonio nods vigorously and starts coughing. Magdala jumps off her stool and shoves the letter and envelope into the pocket of her apron. Silent, she hands over a fresh handkerchief, waits to see how bad the fit will be, then walks to the other side of the bed to shut the blinds, the missing ones like empty teeth in an old smile.

"I was crawling in the dirt and..."

"Tony, the war is over."

No, he tries to tell her, no, no. He can't get it out; only the coughs. The fire swells in his lungs. Tonio wants to build himself a shelter in the garden, beside the zucchini, the firm and large vessels almost as tall as the stakes, wants to become one of them, wrapped in tough wax, plucked ripe. He has a plan, wants to tell Magdala he has a plan, if only he could just finish his dream uninterrupted. If only he could have wind, maybe the sheets would move and someone would see he has already surrendered. When things move, people notice them, he thinks. Let me dig my hole.

Magda picks up the plastic meal tray and turns to leave. "You need anything, Papa?"

"A hole in the dirt."

Magdala stops at the door, her back to Tonio. "Don't say that Tony, please..." She closes it behind her.

Tonio wants to see the girls today, but knows that he won't. He said too much and said it all wrong, and he curses the dreams that keep his words away, hoarding them, shoving them deeper inside his body. The little bombs are like my words, he thinks, shooting inside all hot, fiery and useless, poking me in the ribs and thighs, making me feel but not tell. Rosa and Teresa. He wants to see them. They are good girls to their papa, but Teresa's too pretty and Rosa knows about the dreams. He can tell. She dreams too, but he doesn't know what she dreams of, and neither of them could ever find the right words to share them. She always says, "Sweet dreams, Papa. Sweet ones today," and Tonio wants to take her in his arms and kiss her, even though she is too big, and sometimes he can't control his hands so the girls aren't supposed to touch him in case they get hit. So, instead, they wave to each other, nod and once in a while Rosa combs his hair. Tonio tells Magdala what to say to them, especially if he thinks they're in trouble. He tells her to warn Teresa about boys and Rosa about crossing the street. "Teach Rosa how to do things for herself," he says. "Soon you'll need her." And Magdala has been teaching her all about the chores. She's a good woman. She knows about these things.

Tonio never sees the girls in the dreams, but thinks that sometimes they can see him from the window. Maybe they want to see what he'll do, if he can make it, and when he thinks this, he can feel their eyes on him like rays. Sometimes the girls hang the shirts on the line for their mamma. They help out, see the stains, wash them out. All have been passed the recipe. They know the things he can't help doing. Know about the laundry. Some days he can smell the sting of all that salt as they pass his door in the corridor. But he doesn't see their hands in his dreams, rubbing out his shirts and sheets, cold under the water. The hands that need to work are his own. He is the one in charge of getting out.

Good shirts, all white and strong, no holes. Tonio holds onto the one he is wearing, stripping the front off his wine-sweaty chest, crunching his hands into fists. Pulling, rocking on the bed, he tries to rip it. The top, he notices, has a stronger stitch than the bottom, so he switches his mode of attack, yanking the cloth down and up, until his fingernails hurt and he can't catch his breath. The shirt is swollen but undefeated, and he is coughing hard again. Rosa knocks. By the height of the sound, he can tell that she is using her leg to hit against the wood.

"Papa? Papa? You need Mamma?"

He waves her away, but the door is between them. Alone. He wants to be alone. Alone with his white shirt. But he can hear Rosa's uneven walk shuffling down the hallway, and soon she is calling for Mamma, Mamma. Magdala charges in, shutting the door on Rosa.

Tonio starts to cry.

"Have you had an accident? Don't cry, Papa. I can wash the sheets." Nodding, he lets her lift his frame, bend him and turn him sideways until all the corners of the sheets are untucked. Then a hard tug and a quick smell, her nose like a small animal's. Opening the door, she hands the sheets to Rosa, the white middle stained yellow, the left corner red. Rosa trudges downstairs and Tonio knows she will start the rigorous rubbing before placing the sheets in the washer. He also knows he won't be given any more wine to sip.

Tonio holds out his arm. He wants to touch Magdala, tell her everything is fine, that she doesn't understand, the dream will end and soon. Wants to feel her strong cheeks, bury himself in the grey ribbons of her hair. She walks over, kisses him on the forehead, wipes away her own sweat underneath her nose. Upset that he has failed to keep everything white once again, he turns his head on his pillow and pretends to fall asleep. Magdala gives the rest of the room a quick inspection, checks the wastebasket, then the four corners, lingering for a moment on the photographs on the wall as if deciding whether or not to move them, then exits, shutting the door. Tonio stares out the cracked blinds to the garden, wonders where all the fire and water will go, what they will take with them. One day, perhaps soon, in his fits of coughing, he'll know, and rid himself of both dreams.

RUST STAINS:
Apply lemon juice and salt; then place in oven.

She is surprised it hasn't died yet. Endlessly, every day, it turns and turns; then rests its weary frame at night, though it seems to be on its last legs, moaning and trudging along, wide torso churning.

Having insisted on helping with the wash, Teresa waits for the spin cycle to stop. With Mamma's back trouble it's getting difficult for her to carry the loads herself, even if the stairs are few to the basement. Soaking in salt in the metal basin are Papa's sheets, turning the white water pink. She will scrub them with more detergent before inserting them in the next load. Soon the wash will be entirely Rosa's job, when Teresa marries and leaves the house, although this will not happen before Papa dies. But she has her ring, her promise, her simple silver band and four-karat diamond, in the bottom drawer of her dresser, in the pocket of her good pair of black pants she wears only to funerals. Until she wears those pants to bid Papa a final goodbye, it helps him to have his girls in the house.

She showed Mamma the ring a month ago, two weeks after Wilhelm proposed, when they were out drying the laundry. But she hasn't shown Papa the ring, or Rosa. Rosa wouldn't be able to keep her mouth shut, they decided, and Papa still likes to think of the girls as the little children they were when he was first confined to the bedroom. No one wants to upset Papa. Mamma does the dirty work, dumping the pan if Papa is able to warn her in time, or else cleaning his underwear. Lifting his frame, she arranges him into positions for eating and sleeping, and reads letters from back home out loud to him until they are both choked up and Papa coughing. There is blood sometimes, too, that Mamma tries to hide. Teresa worries about where the blood comes from, which part of Papa hurts the most. At first she thought it was blood on Papa's sheet, like on the clothes she threw away, and she was prepared to throw out Papa's sheets too. But, upon closer inspection, the sweet linger of the smell informed her otherwise. So, she filled the basin with hot water and now watches it swoosh in waves beside the rumble of the machine.

When Teresa is alone in her room, she likes to hold the engagement ring in her hand, but then returns it guiltily to the darkness of her drawers when she hears Papa's coughing. No dreaming yet of what is to come. Not that she's anxious to leave yet exactly either. Wilhelm is a nice man, it's not that. And handsome. They met at his restaurant, *House of Rio*, a diner where she and her friends sometimes stop for coffee and cake after school. Wilhelm was washing the countertops and offered her an extra slice of carrot cake. Then he started picking her up from school. Lots of her friends knew about it, about her romance with this man almost ten years older, and then a man at the restaurant, a regular customer—the one she won't name anymore—offered her a lift. She agreed, but he didn't take her home, not right away, and she was scared and tried to fight him, but…and Mamma saw her get out of the…Wilhelm is a nice man. He has gentle brown eyes and hairy arms and his hands are tender, even comforting on her neck and shoulders, or up and down her legs. He promises to help her open a store, promises to help Rosa. Her friends are all excited that she will be the first among them to get married. One even said it's smart of her to get out of the whole college and university mess by plunking herself right into a family business. And maybe it is, though it's weird to think that many of her friends will be in school when she's married and washing restaurant dishes, chopping vegetables, buying cakes and then, later, having babies. How will she be able to do the things in the restaurant or her store plus all the things Mamma does: cleaning, cooking, changing, gardening? For now, at least, she is just the helper with the wash, her papa's little girl.

"Good girl," Mamma said when Teresa produced the silver ring with the small diamond, warm from clutching it tightly in her pocket. "Just make sure you're not showing before the wedding."

"Mamma! I'm not pregnant."

Mamma looked surprised, but obviously believed her, the expression on her face changing from stern practicality to a wan hope.

"Then we can wait, Tera?"

Teresa agreed.

And Teresa can wait too, wait as long as she has that ring tucked away: her promise. Wilhelm won't betray her. She visits him everyday at the restaurant, and he is, by all accounts, a man in love. "Family first," he said, when she told him about waiting for Papa. "So many young people don't understand that anymore. I'm glad you do." Now she can still go to school, to the dances, shopping with friends, and take Rosa to the park or help her with sewing. And she knows her mother is happy she won't be going to college or university to make a career for herself. "Girls are silly to want to act like men. They have no idea what men go through. The wars," Mamma told her, "the wars could happen again, and then who will watch out for the children?" Teresa likes some of the old ways. Yes, she likes the idea of marriage and doesn't want to be one of *those* girls, but there are also so many rules: the rule that makes Rosa stay in the house and take care of Mamma after Papa dies, the rule that Mamma can't put Papa in a hospital, the rules about babies, the many babies she will be expected to have, unless she has one like Rosa.

When Teresa dreams about the wedding, she dreams about how everyone will dance, even Rosa, and the machinations behind her turn into music, the soaked sheet into a massive tablecloth. Mamma will smile, clap her hands and grab on to a chair thinking Papa is beside her. Then a tall white cake rises to the front of her mind, along with frilly decorations, and proud invitations, especially the ones to Mamma's and Papa's families back in Portugal who won't be able to come. Her hair will be worn up, in a twist, and she'll carry white lilies in her hands. Sure, they will have to skimp on a few things, there has never been a lot of money and Wilhelm wants to put money aside for the future clothing store, but traditions are still traditions and the nice thing is she knows she will have all the necessities no matter what happens. Mamma says so and when Papa is gone...

"Look, Tera!"

Shaking herself out of her dream, Teresa pulls off her rubber laundry gloves. Rosa offers up a skirt for her inspection, a green paisley pattern with wide swirls Teresa recognizes as the old coarse fabric from the basement curtains.

"Look at the stitches, Tera!"

Teresa examines the cloth, turning it over and inside out. The stitches are firm when she tugs. Obviously nervous, humming to herself and tapping her good leg, Rosa beams when the stitches hold.

"Very good. Really good," Teresa tells her, the spin cycle rolling on behind them, and it is. Rosa is good with her hands, learns quickly if you show her exactly how. There are times Teresa thinks that Rosa has the most talent, and could make a wonderful wife, if she just wasn't the way she is. In a certain light, Rosa appears almost grandmotherly, her thighs loose like after child-bearing, her breasts down to her stomach if she isn't wearing a bra. It makes Teresa wonder what kind of children she will have, if she might resemble Rosa more afterwards.

"I made it for you to dance in. Put it on."

Smiling, Teresa slips the skirt underneath her dress, pinning the hem of her dress upside down under her armpits. Rosa's firm hands zip it up in the back. The skirt is a little formless for Teresa's taste, and the pattern is faded lime in a couple of spots, but it fits and rests pleasantly at the knee.

"Thanks, Rosa," Teresa says, taking it off and placing it in the laundry basket she will use later to carry the clean clothes.

Rosa sways her arms and pounds her foot on the ground to the thumping of the washing machine until the strap on her brace comes off. Grimacing, Rosa bends down to fix it, the canvas strip tight in her fist like rope.

"I'm not too good at dancing."

"Sure you are, Rosa. You'll dance soon."

When Rosa has tied the strap back securely, Teresa picks up some wooden pins. "You did a fine job, Rosa. Now Mamma could use some help outside."

Rosa accepts the pins as they drop into her hand. Teresa waves her on and Rosa obeys. Mamma's worn running shoes pass by the window.

The washer goes into a fit, the little shelf holding the cleaners suffering a tiny earthquake. But Teresa knows the routine. It always does this moments before resting. Coughing and spitting up water, banging against the concrete wall, it sweats itself dry. Then there's the silence that means it's all over. But, this time, before the silence arrives, Teresa abandons her dreaming and runs upstairs to check on Papa.

Saint Candice

Catherine Hernandez

Huff, huff, huff, huff. Candice ran as fast as she could toward a TTC bus approaching a shelter in the distance. She ran past Chanaman Roti Stand, the Rastas pausing their meal of corn bread and pepper sauce to watch her whiz by. Huff, huff, huff, huff. She ran past Madame Quan's Nail Salon, the smell of acrylics filling Candice's lungs. Her legs were a wind-up toy, rhythmic and determined, until she arrived at her destination.

The doors of the bus met halfway—with Candice's kilt in between. An animal with its tail snagged in a trap, she pulled at the grey and purple tartan hard enough to thrust her into the lap of the bus driver.

"Watch your step!" the driver said, wiping her thighs as though Candice had left a stain.

Candice reached into her pocket and was surprised to find a token. Her student tickets would have been useless since her ID card wasn't in her pocket. It was gone. It lay on the black asphalt, her dowdy mug shot staring at the sky.

Candice wiped away the fog from inside the bus window as the bus pulled away. She could see the crowd of people that had begun to gather. At its centre, the man dressed in green stared blankly at his unexpected audience.

Candice turned her attention to the people on board the bus. A young mother with her stroller. A teenage boy's head bobbing in his sleep. The other commuters kept their gaze transfixed on the horizon. Had they seen?

◆ ◆ ◆

"Darling," said Candice's mother, Sugar, as she stood precariously atop a stool. Sugar passed her daughter a Styrofoam plate covered in a mixture of sticky cooking oil and fly carcasses and then gestured with her lips towards the garbage bin. Candice obliged.

While her mother continued her warfare on the flies, Candice looked with disdain at the messy kitchen.

Whether or not Candice was telling the truth, the Garcia family had been host to many visitors over the spring. Who would have thought that of all the people the Mother Mary in her blue glory would appear to, it would be Candice Garcia. All these pious Doñas, altars shrewn with dusty, beaded rosaries awaiting a sign from the Almighty, candles ablaze, knees chaffed—and yet nothing but silence for them.

Picture it: Candice, the shame of the Garcia family, folding laundry at the Morningside Mall Coin and Clean, when the Virgin Mother appeared. How peculiar!

The Garcia family's kitchen was overwhelmed with Styrofoam plates bent under the weight of delectable dishes offered by visitors. Lechon, diniguan, pancit palabok: the enticing scent of Filipino food, now rancid and sour, left nothing but flies in its wake.

Everyone was eager to see this new conduit of the Lord.

"How gracious of God to pay us a visit!" they would cry, smiling tightly around the lips.

Perhaps it hadn't been wise of God to choose such an unruly girl who now grimaced at the eager hands wanting to touch her and who refused to give any details of the blessed encounter. Being a prophet was not easy. One did not choose this role. You simply did what was asked of you. Each detail counted. What was Mary wearing? Is the laundromat a holy place? Is the end near? Nothing. What an ungrateful girl.

How often had these women given a toonie or even a crisp five-dollar bill when the offering basket came about? Why not their own daughters? Out of all the chaste Filipinas in the St. Joseph's congregation, why Candice?

The community was well aware of her reputation. Just the sight of her cinnamon-coloured buttocks peeking seductively under her Saint Theresa kilt had the community crossing themselves. The women prayed that God would somehow save her; the men prayed that God would save *them.*

Sugar and her husband, Benny, prayed for God to save their demon child. Sugar would be seen every Saturday lighting a candle in the apse of the Saint Joseph's cathedral, kneeling for hours in prayer.

"God, please help my daughter find her way. God please make her wear proper panties under her kilt!" she'd say into her interlaced fingers, tears soaking her wrists. Perhaps her prayers had been answered.

• • •

Although Emerald Isles Market evoked images of green grocers tipping their Derby hats with the end of a *shillelagh*, the place was run by a Portuguese family, the De Sousas. The Irish, who were the predominant community back in the days of the market's beginnings, had melted into Scarborough's cultural pot. The area was now a mad Bollywood musical come to life, where Hindu temples sit adjacent to Halal meat stores and Tamil video counters set up shop next to Vietnamese pho restaurants.

And there, standing in the midst of Emerald Isles' barren parking lot, clad in Frosted Lucky Charms green, was Gino, the shopping cart collector. His tie was caught underneath one of the cart's child seats—again. Amidst a sea of metal lattice, he tried to pull himself free, but to no avail.

His cousin, Giuseppe, approached him, his apron stained with blood from the meat section. Without pomp and circumstance, Giuseppe took out a pocket knife from his apron, cut Gino's tie free and said, "Get back to work."

Gino waved like a giddy child as he watched his cousin re-enter the premises.

Just then, he saw a teenage boy flying out of the market, pushing a shopping cart. The boy wore a trucker-style baseball cap, its visor turning left and right as he looked cautiously behind him.

The sound of the cart's wheels screeching along the asphalt made the hair on Gino's forearms stand on end and he waved the boy down.

"Hey, thanks!" he called to the boy running towards him. "No, that's okay. Just there is fine."

The boy didn't stop.

"Whoa!" Gino said with a nervous laugh, when the boy didn't stop in front of him. Or at the entrance sign of the parking lot. "Whoa!"

"Stop!"

Gino whipped his head around to see where the voice came from. A young girl with a very short skirt ran towards the boy. In her arms she carried bags of Frito Lays and bulk bags of chocolate bars. No shopping bags. She dumped her loot into the cart and the twosome began running at high speed.

"Hey!" said Bobby, one of the cashiers who came running out of the store in pursuit; his flood-length slacks making his strides into pony trots. "Fuck, Gino! Run after them!"

Like a racing horse at the sound of a bullet, Gino obliged—with blinders on.

◆ ◆ ◆

Lipsticks turned around on a Lazy Susan–type display. It was Revlon's latest Super Moist Lip collection. But Candice's eyes were elsewhere. She stared at the back of the sales clerk whose name (according to her tag) was Lisa. Lisa was busy putting out a cosmetic sales fire.

"But are they tested on animals?" asked a fifteen-year-old girl with braces. Her friends shared her look of disapproval.

"Yeah," added another girl. "'Cuz if it is, we're not buying it. It's the only way we can stop them from killing animals. You know, with our buying power."

Lisa inhaled. "Okay, girls." She positioned her torso so that she could look over the counter. "Take a look at your shoes."

Confused, the girls looked down at their penny loafers and then back at Lisa. "Leather." Lisa spoke like a lawyer delivering her final monologue. "Leather comes from cows. And a cow had to die in order for you to have those shoes."

"Oh," the girls collectively sighed.

"Now, do you gals want to see Revlon's latest *Super Moist Lip* collection?"

The girls giggled with delight, the weight of their buying power shifting to the pink and sparkly political right.

Lisa turned around to find the carousel of lipsticks. She didn't notice the gaping hole that the shade "Liquid Garnet" once occupied.

Candice left the store in a flash.

The feel of the lipstick's cool plastic was turning into molten lava inside her sweatshirt pocket. She could barely feel her legs anymore; her knees were like rusty hinges. One voice inside her head told her to walk as fast as possible, while another told her to walk normally. With flushed cheeks, she ran to the nearest darkened corner of the mall to take her first breath in ten minutes.

"Where are you going?"

Candice was jolted by a voice both gruff and uneven. It was Shawn, resident Bad Boy of Pope John Paul II High School. And there were an awful lot of bad boys already there. His trucker baseball cap was stiff and new, but his face was the surface of the moon.

"You look kind of nervous," he added with a sly grin. "You weren't stealing or anything, were you?"

Candice inched her way towards the exit but Shawn intercepted her. "I saw what you did."

"So?"

"So? Didn't your mother ever tell you that stealing is wrong?"

"What's your problem?"

"My problem is," Shawn said, while looking around him conspiratorially, "you owe me. Big time."

"Why?"

"Because. You know why the guards didn't catch you walking at a hundred miles per hour trying to look normal with your fucking hands in your pocket?" His face was inches away from her. "Because I distracted them. I was watching you all along as you were turning those lipsticks around and around wondering when you were going to make your move. And when you did I asked the guards some stupid question. I fucking saved your ass."

Candice's face was burning. "Thanks."

"So what's it gonna be?"

"Excuse me?"

"What do I get in return for saving you from jail?"

"Listen, alright, whatever you heard about me isn't true. I don't do that shit, okay?"

"Hey, hey!" said Shawn, putting his arm around Candice suggestively. "I don't mean that. Come on. I mean…I didn't mean anything like that."

• • •

One of Candice's earliest memories is of her first Communion. While walking in a lineup towards the altar, she rocked back and forth in her white dress shoes to get a glimpse of Father Michael. But the plains of crinoline from the girls ahead kept her from seeing the priest placing the Eucharist in everyone's mouth.

When she finally approached Father Michael, he sternly told her to hold out her tongue. On it, he placed the dry papery wafer. Candice remembers the sensation of her saliva being absorbed into the unleavened bread. *I am eating the body of Christ,* she thought to herself. *And he tastes like popcorn.*

She returned to her seat.

"It tastes like popcorn, doesn't it?" said a man who sat beside her in the pew. Her legs dangled from her seat, but his sandaled feet were like tree trunks on the red carpet.

"Kinda," Candice said, smiling at the sun shining behind the man's head. "He must have been a big man."

"Why?"

"Everyone is eating him," Candice said, pointing to the Communion line with her lace glove.

"No," said the man, thoughtfully stroking his beard. "They just slice me really thinly."

Candice laughed—not because he was funny but because he said it in a way that meant he was telling a joke. Like the people in the *Cosby Show.*

"Gotta go," the man said, playfully tapping his knuckle onto the white patent leather, as if he was knocking on a door. As he got up, he stretched. "My mom is calling me."

Candice looked about the congregation, wondering who his mother was. "You'll meet her one day. She says she wants to talk to you."

By the time she looked back at him, he was gone.

• • •

Shawn's arm never left Candice's shoulder. Not when leaving the mall. Not while they strolled into the deepest depths of Orton Park. Against her will, she tagged along, silent and afraid.

Shawn's basement was littered with clothes. The teen odour was rank and solid. The pair entered, linked shoulder to shoulder, into the darkness of the room. Lights flickered on a TV exposing the debris on the shag carpet. Video games that were once stacked on top of one another lay like toppled dominos. Candice navigated the floor—a war zone of underwear and half-eaten bread crusts—with her toes clenched. And what was that crunchy sound with every step? Candice shuddered at the thought of pizza crumbs stuck to the bottoms of her knee-high socks.

Shawn opened up his fridge door and peered inside. A cube of butter sat alone on a mildew-stained shelf. Time to go shopping.

"You heard me. I'm hungry." Shawn said, while stapling down some frayed carpet.

Candice swallowed hard before muttering, "I won't do it."

"What's the difference between a few bags of chips and lipstick?"

"I won't do it. I don't want to do that again."

With staple gun still in hand, he got up and pressed his chest into Candice's, his gaze menacing.

"You think you're gonna go to jail or something? Am I asking you to kill somebody?" He took a breath and held her chin firmly. Lovingly. His gaze still menacing. "Emerald Isles is a fucking mom and pop shop. No one will even notice. They'll be too busy doing what those wops do."

Candice looked longingly at Shawn's front door; a tempting line of sunlight peeping across its threshold.

"Fine."

• • •

Having only room for one thought at a time in his simple brain, Gino ran, as ordered, towards the teens with the shopping cart.

Had he had room for one more thought, perhaps he would have heard the sound of the St. Malachy school bus driving towards him, its seats filled with rowdy youth coming back from a school trip to the Hockey Hall of Fame.

If there was room for three thoughts he would have felt the displacement of air between him and the bus's front fender; the feel of metal against his shoulder, the feel of his own arm crushing into his rib cage.

And if there was room for four thoughts, he would have found it peculiar to have heard the sound of angels singing slightly odd.

But there was only room for one thought: Run after the teens. That's when the bus ran into him.

◆ ◆ ◆

"Oh my God! Oh my God!" Candice looked around for help. Shawn was no where to be seen. "Jesus! Oh God!"

The hefty bus driver hobbled towards them.

"What happened?" the driver cried, her hands cupping blood at her forehead.

"Oh God!" Candice held him; her arms shaking under his weight. "Please don't die. Please don't die. Please don't die," she repeated again and again until the words began to run together like one long song.

The students on the bus began to empty out, surrounding Candice and the man in green.

The warmth of Candice's hands on Gino's skin suddenly became unbearable. Her grasp was tight and her tears were steamy like hot syrup.

"Ow!" Gino doubled over. "Ow! You're hurting me."

Candice watched Gino suddenly stand. He looked back at the glow around Candice's head and said, "My tummy. It's turning. I can taste it in my mouth."

"You should sit down," said the bus driver. "Sit down before you barf."

Gino took one step toward Candice, then fell to his knees and onto his back again.

Candice looked at her hands. No blood.

"What the fuck?" She touched Gino's arm in disbelief. No blood. No break. A living, breathing man. Even though she had watched him catapult through the air.

"How did you do that?" The driver said, turning to watch Candice run at full speed, just in time to catch a TTC bus driving westward.

◆ ◆ ◆

Candice sat on a single seat close to the front of the bus. She didn't want to sit at the back. Not today.

She watched the bus pull away from the crowd. She watched the traffic go by until the noise of the tire screeching slowly left her head. She welcomed the hum of the bus's engine. A young mother with her stroller. A teenage boy's head bobbing in his sleep. The others with their eyes transfixed on the horizon.

She watched a lady take out a book from her purse and a highlighter for note taking. Beside the lady, a teenage boy was looking over her shoulder.

"Whad are you reating?" the boy asked at the top of his voice while rocking back and forth.

The lady cringed at the sight of his slack-eyed face, just inches away from her shoulder. "I'm reading a book."

"Whah kinda book? I lye comic books."

"It's a…uh, non-fiction book." The commuters sniggered.

"Whatzit called?" he persisted.

The lady exhaled.

"It's…it's called…*How to Love Yourself.*"

The commuters sniggered.

"Hmmm," said the boy. He pushed up his thick glasses and rubbed his beardless chin in thought. *"I know howtah lub myself."*

The lady rolled her eyes. What would a retard know?

But Candice was smiling. She smiled all the way home.

Poems

Nermeen Mouftah

62

AMAL SINGS AT THE CHRISTMAS PAGEANT

Amal stands in front of the gymnasium,
she doesn't fidget, she stands straight.

Jeremy hisses, Why does your cousin always have to sing?
and I shrug my shoulders. The gymnasium is almost quiet,
it's Christmas and students whisper like crinkling wrapping paper.
Girls blow greasy bangs off their foreheads
when they see her on stage. Her. Again.

When Amal opens her mouth
a crystal liquid pours out

O HOLY NIGHT

The audience wants to go home
and drink warm syrupy drinks with step-fathers and half-sisters.
The audience sat through Mrs. Ormiston's choir
and the middle school jazz club, but it is for Amal
that the fluorescent lights courteously stop their buzz.

THE STARS ARE BRIGHTLY SHINING,
IT IS THE NIGHT OF THE DEAR SAVIOUR'S BIRTH.

They know we don't celebrate Christmas
but so far, no one is poking me and asking me why
she is singing about Jesus.
No one wants to know, or maybe they don't care,
or don't know the difference.

LONG LAY THE WORLD IN SIN AND ERROR PINING.

She doesn't see any of us. She hits every note perfectly.
Teachers stand against the walls with candied smiles,
they don't notice that the world hates Amal,
that the world wants her to shut up and get off the stage
and stop wearing lipstick, who does she think she is?

A THRILL OF HOPE THE WEARY WORLD REJOICES

Angela is looking at me and wants me to say something
about Amal, so she can laugh,
she wants me to tell the story
about what body parts she shaves
and she wants the boys around us to hear.

On stage, Amal is there, at the point in the song
where she will win or lose, except she always wins.
To prepare herself for the note, she is looking up
at the rafters of the gymnasium,
trying to bring the song that high

FALL ON YOUR KNEES!

OH, HEAR THE ANGEL VOICES!

O NIGHT DIVINE

Nobody misses it. It is now Amal's song
and if these kids were honest, they'd be crying.

O NIGHT DIVINE

Some more people are looking at me
and I understand that I'm going to be partly responsible for this.
Her eyes are still steady on some point high above our heads
as she sings out her finale,
the one that says, Fuck you, merry Christmas,
I can sing your goddamned songs better than any of you
stringy-haired, white-assed retards.

O NIGHT DIVINE

The one thing about Amal is how when she finishes
she will walk off the stage and sit among us
and Angela will squeeze her shoulder and say, that was amazing!
and Amal will smile and take the compliment lightly
because she doesn't care what Angela says.

O NIGHT DIVINE

Angela leans over to me, What is she staring at on the ceiling?
she makes dramatic efforts to imitate Amal
and find something on the ceiling,
pulling her face up towards the rafters,
she says, I don't see anything up there, do you?

When she finishes, the gymnasium
is the click of her shoes, too formal for a Christmas pageant,
the click down the wooden stage steps,
the hesitation, and then, at last, the applause
we all know we are responsible for.

A RULE FOR GETTING THROUGH THE CITY

The rule is: don't give money to Rose
when she gets on the subway and asks you for it.

The TTC man will tell you to put your change away
and Rose will ignore him, or not hear him,

and the woman sitting beside you will ignore him
when she pulls out some coins to put in Rose's hand.

The TTC man will say that Rose is always
getting on the subway to beg for change

and THAT is against the rules.
The woman beside you will say, I know this woman.

Somewhere else you see someone stand
to give Rose some change.

The rule is simple. It has something to do
with not making people feel uncomfortable.

Rose is clamouring down the train and dividing
the group: those who give

and those who do not. There are those
who sympathize with the TTC man and the glory of rules

and those who simply do not give (for all of the reasons
that there are not to give) and those who empty their change

into Rose's hand because fuck the TTC and their rules.
There are those who give because Rose is black and so are they,

those who do not give because Rose is black and so are they;
those who give because they can smell her.

There are those who give
because this is a revolution going on here,

something is getting done here. Rose is walking among us,
not giving a shit that she's causing people to disagree

and whip out morality and politics on the evening ride home,
when surely we were raised to be more polite.

RECOVERING DISTANCE

We are speaking, the topic political,
and you are wondering
why I always think I am right.
You say, *I am trying to hear*
where you are coming from,
as though we are miles apart
and this is the most exhausting task.
I assume you are wondering about my bias
so I unpack all of my titles
and lay them before you
like a Bedouin merchant with silver trinkets.
Now you look at me as though it is 1942
and I am speaking Japanese,
my mouth moving, hands gesticulating.
You hear me say, *I am right,*
I am right, I am right.
But what I actually say is this:
I live in Canada, yet every day I hear
bombs fall over my head.

Poems
Marlene Goldman

69

TOTAL IMMERSION

The guy in the tight, black Speedo
(shine over the crotch)
is ready to dive;

another Russian Jew,
new to the community pool,
unsure of how to say "Make way!,"
makes his announcement nonetheless
cannonball style:

"I am here
in your country. Like it
or not."

In the deep end,
suddenly I'm under
a flying immigrant
bent on total immersion.

Two leaps are made
in the same instant;

my body, like his,
performs a dazzling trick:

I jump into the arms of the lifeguard
swimming laps beside me.

(Clearly, what the young
Russian wanted and what I needed,
still under my father's roof,
was only to be got by leaping.)

Later, the lifeguard confessed
he'd never been grabbed
or grabbed anyone
who wasn't drowning.

Five years older and charming,
he was smug as a fisherman
who reeled in a day's catch
on an unbaited line.

At my parents' table,
to their horror,
he held and stroked me
like an animal.

At night, after they retired,
he would escort me
to the sofa and hump me
through my summer dress.

Everything
was utterly changed,
new and unfathomable:

the weight of his body,
the zipper at his crotch,
grinding against my hip, the wet
salt-stain blooming through.

And when, finally, I persuaded him
to go all the way, we drove
to his parents' house and crept
into his sister's room. He lay
a towel on the bed, imagining
waves of blood.

Afterward, my hair tangled
in the wrought-iron filagree,
I was stunned and gutted.
He boasted: "Give me half an hour,
and we'll do it again."

Months later, he fucked me from behind;
this time, both of us were braced—
he squatted against the wall;
I gripped the bathroom sink—

a lost country and its pleasures
locked in the body
from childhood,
erupted.

The Russian stopped
frequenting the pool,
ending all embarrassment,
though I wondered,
did he ever learn English?
And when I announced
to the lifeguard:
I'd met someone else,
he lowered me wordlessly
to the hard ground and lay
on top of me. One hundred
and sixty-five pounds
of adamant flesh
on my flesh.

Released,
I rose as docile as I'd been
in my father's house.

Though he handed me
an engagement ring and spoke
warmly of the rooms
he'd build for me
in our house,
we parted as abruptly
as we'd met.

I aimed and landed the blow—
my fist to his unguarded heart—
in a stream of traffic
at Spadina and College,
near the market,
where everyone arrives
after the diaspora.

THE STAYMAN CONVENTION

1. One No Trump
Our conversation begins hours before I visit,
with this late-afternoon ritual, with the first
drops of sweat on my skin. To join you,
I must follow convention: Respect.
Deference. Uphold the image of a father
who's strong and in control.

It was the same when your mother died.
Though you left the bathroom door open,
and I found you sobbing on the toilet,
it wasn't the nakedness, but the raw, wet sounds
caught in your throat that mystified, shamed.
Swiping at your cheeks, you murmured,
"I shouldn't be crying.
Me, a grown man."

Now at the gym, heart racing, I pedal
a stationary bike. I learned everything here
from you about strength, control and winning.
Like a child locked to a rocking horse,
head down, I am aiming for the prize.

When well-meaning women approach
to offer comfort: "It's such a difficult time
for your family. Please, give everyone my love,"
I don't lift my head or open myself
to their unasked questions.

2. Two Clubs
Alone in the hospital room it's easier:
the faded mint-green gown,
the nursery-white bed with bars
we both ignore.
You ask me only to read
from *Bridge Made Easy*
and I bend over the cheap paper,
recite the dark words.

You're intent on mastering
the Stayman Convention.
I read this chapter over and over—
noting how vulnerable you are:
your wavy, uncombed hair the colour of toffee,
eyes slightly out of focus (lack of sleep
or something they've given you).

But you open with the usual complaint:
"The food here stinks."
I'm tempted to pass, but instead I declare:
"I'll bring you something—anything you like."
"Don't go to the trouble," you say,
    having nothing to ask for,
    thinking I have nothing to offer.

3. Two Diamonds
When I was a child,
your thick, callused fingers
seized the laces at the throat of my skates
and pulled them tight—impossibly tight—
you wove two columns of diamonds.
The strength of your hands
immobilized my ankles
so I could stand.

4. Two Hearts
I can count the times
you've spoken openly and honestly;
though I still believe it's possible,
even this late in the game.
I imagine you shone clear as a child,
and I could have asked you anything—
the way I ask friends about their lives:
"What did you eat for breakfast as a kid?"

Before this terrible enchantment, I imagine
you were capable of offering stories
about waffles with whipped cream brought to you in bed,
or biscuits with chocolate sauce,
or terrible, gelatinous oatmeal
spooned reluctantly from the bowl.

Once I wrote a letter from camp:
"What do you remember
 about where you were born?"
In your precise hand, you replied:
"The smell of piss and straw and
 being hungry all the time.
 Never ask me again."

By the time I was born,
you'd been through the war
and lost all appetite for remembering.

5. Two Spades
Once, when I was a teenager, you surprised us all
by becoming someone else.
Drunk at a family function, for the first time,
you paraded stories about fighting overseas—
English girls with peaches-and-cream skin, tea dances,
waltzing under elegant canopies, marching in uniform
across London Bridge.

You confessed, in those days, to calling yourself
Mr. White. You loved how the name took you everywhere—
you with your sticking-out ears, your wrong name, you loved
how this name opened every door (after what you'd seen, you were willing
to try new ways, you knew that work wouldn't set you free).

Even behind the alias, you suspected
your girlfriend's father was on to you: he made Jew-jokes
over port and cigars, waited for your response.
You held your ground, told one yourself.

In the middle of this story, you leaned toward me,
drunk and self-conscious: "You think you're a clever one,
but you're never going to know me." As if I weren't playing
on your side, as if I knew something
as harmless as a conversation
could break you.

The Man Who Built Walls and Tore Them Down

Kerri Sakamoto

An excerpt from a novel-in-progress,
The Mongolian Spot

It was the first time I'd sat down with Frank since moving out five years earlier. More might have passed were it not for Yuri killing himself. I recall thinking spring was the season I would've chosen, too. It was the first time in a long while that I'd relinquished my resistance to thinking of Frank as my father, instead of simply a man whose existence was parallel to mine, and only incidentally connected through people I loved.

We had faced each other in the crematorium of course, two months before. We'd watched Yuri's mother gather up five pieces of her only son's bones with disposable wooden chopsticks—not wanting his bones to feel the coldness of metal—with such dexterity it seemed she'd done it before. She hadn't, but she would do it a few more times, outliving her widowed sister and even Frank. She performed in calm, in silence, except near the end when she whispered Yuri's name as if to coax him from his hiding place. I'd always found it ironic, my father giving my older half-brother a name that sounded both Jewish and Japanese when Yuri was the full-blooded one. And that was long before my father met his second wife, my mother, who came from a family of survivors.

I met Frank in his office with its floor-to-ceiling windows and the CN Tower—the jewel in his crown and his sceptre—right there behind him amid a blanched royal blue sky. Beyond that, water: the lake he liked to pretend was sea, and the surrounding land, the views to it he'd been buying up through some scheme or other, block by block, for years. He looked terrible. I felt pity for him but then reminded myself that he always looked that way, with his heavy-lidded, uncannily un-Asian eyes that he refused, for as long as possible, to shield with a pair of glasses; he had a protuberant mouth whose sloppiness constantly betrayed him. His nose claimed all his face and none of it, sprawling across it and receding into the crag of his profile. A journalist once called him a *beau-laid* and it rang true: his bravado transformed him; the sheer audacity of a man so undeniably unattractive, always thrusting his face into the spotlight. A Japanese face at that, even back after the war when it was still the face of the enemy. If he winced at later seeing himself in magazines, on television or in the mirror, Frank was also reassured by the ubiquitousness of his own image and his works as they were transforming the city.

My aunt Aki said that like me, he'd never really resembled a child even when he was one. My grandmother called him a monkey. He could never sit still, never at home in his skin. It didn't help that his sisters teased and convinced him he had a different father from them, that his blood was different, a darker red, and thicker. They pricked and squeezed his finger while he slept then added ink to show him in the morning. Aunt Aki said she heard talk among the neighbours back on Vancouver Island of my grandmother's lascivious ways before marrying my grandfather. It was said that Frank's real father might've been some kind of Buddhist shaman, or of a lowly class. My father had been running from his own ghost ever since his younger brother died in one of the internment camps that the Japanese in Canada, foreign or Canadian born, had been banished to after Pearl Harbor was bombed. Frank was terrified he'd been marked for early death like his younger brother, whose Mongolian spot had stayed from birth to the day he died at sixteen. The blue-black oval just above the crack of his backside had never disappeared as it should have. No one knew how to explain the spot: it was there when babies were born and usually vanished by age three. The only question about it had always been why white babies didn't have it, too. Frank's spot, like those of my aunts, had come and gone. But he was convinced his might one day reappear.

Frank shrank before his superstitions; those idiosyncratic tremors could shake him to the core. When it came to my birth, Aunt Aki said, "He watched over you until that spot on your behind disappeared when you were two." It was the one thing Aunt Aki told me that I found hard to believe: Frank as a worried, caring father. Yet I could imagine him obsessed with the fate of one inextricably, genetically bound up with him. I asked my aunt about Yuri. His spot was barely there, she'd answered, gone in no time, and I could imagine the oval above his pale infant buttock, little more than a dab of soot to be scrubbed clean with a cloth dampened by mother's spit.

I remember Frank distressed and undone, my mother trying to calm him even as she unravelled with him. He'd bounce on the balls of his feet in one spot and shudder at tearing down a building whose address began or ended in four, or whose digits added up to four because its written Japanese character also meant death. That's when I could see the childish monkey Frank, jumping out of his skin. And yet he wouldn't think twice about the people in the building who might not find another place to live. Only my mother held some chance of assuaging him. She knew what it was to be haunted by the ghosts of ancestors and their primitive burdens; she knew how to slip out from under the weight of the past, at least in the moment. Frank's first wife, Yuri's mother, locked herself in a freighted silence that no doubt unnerved Frank even more.

But it was only in such a moment that my parents could seem like a couple. Most times, the things in common kept them apart. They shared a self-pity they could admit to neither themselves nor each other. They could excuse themselves for anything and others for little because they'd been wronged from birth, singled out for a persecution sewn into their hearts, a secret badge. I could've blamed my mother more for what went wrong between them because she bore it with a knowing if private pride. Frank was oblivious to what he hid from himself. So how could he ever give solace to her or to anyone?

At family barbeques when Yuri was twelve and I was eight, Frank would leap out in front of all the cousins and me to scare us by taking out his top false teeth, emitting a roar from that abyssal black hole of his exceptional mouth. Then he'd pop the dentures back in crookedly, breathing slowly and heavily. It terrified me—the row of inhumanly identical teeth embedded in shiny pink, the hissing exhalations. That mouth and its displaced teeth stalked my dreams. I woke, horrified to have the fear of my own father lurking inside me. I never purged that nightmarish vision of him; in fact, I kept it all these years, nursed it as I finally grasped how unhappy he'd made everyone around him. I kept it to rationalize leaving home at seventeen, and to keep a guilt-laden homesickness at bay, but I suffered for it anyway.

Still, I can't help recalling the clown he was to all my little cousins. He made them giddy, especially when he picked each of them up in turn and swung them in the air, threw them high and caught them just shy of the ground. They whooped and kissed him, not so much oblivious to, but intoxicated by the magic in his monstrousness. He pulled candy from every one of his pockets and envelopes with five-dollar bills tucked inside. As he did, he'd glance my way, as if to say: You see? They like me, why don't you?

I never cried for or because of my father. But when I did cry, somehow, no matter where he was at the time, Yuri would find me. He'd hunt for the place where it hurt, as he did when I cried for my mother when she cried for my father. Yuri would leave me for a moment that seemed an eternity, then return from somewhere—the bathroom or a nearby drugstore—with a box of Band-Aids. He'd offer me rectangles and circles, bandaging my tears, my nose, my mouth; bandaging my arms, my legs, every ticklish inch of me he could until the box was empty and I laughed so hard I peed my pants.

"Saw you once," Frank was now saying, pointing down to the street, his finger circling around an area. "Cleaning the windshield of a car ahead of me. Foot of Spadina. You didn't see me."

"I did."

"That lady didn't pay you a cent."

"Why should she?"

"You did a job. Yuri would say that, right? He dragged you into that business."

I shrugged my shoulders. The shoulders Yuri would squeeze, to tell me he was there, right behind me, all the way. "He told me to go home."

My father swivelled in his chair away from me, eye to eye with his tower, its protruding nerve centre. He hunched over, doing something I couldn't see; for a moment, I thought he might jump up with those teeth to scare me, though he'd probably gotten implants by now. When I was young, I believed that was his tactic for making people give him what he wanted, how he got all that land to build on, to put up fortresses that blocked the sun and walled in the lake so only he could see it. There was dark treachery in it all.

Lately, the newspapers were saying he wanted to do just the opposite: tear down the walls, demolish the hideous expressway that was collapsing anyway, chunk by chunk from the belly of an ossified dinosaur never meant to survive past this century.

It was two years ago that I'd found Yuri living beneath it, right near where Frank saw me at Spadina Quay. It wasn't for long; the end of that summer, Yuri had come back from Amsterdam after his business failed. He'd spent every last penny on the fare home but he wouldn't call Frank. In Amsterdam, he'd fixed up an old boat on a canal near the red-light district and let out bunks to backpacking students. He called it Hostel Waters. Frank, who counted out every niggardly penny he lent to Yuri for start-up, objected to the name. He said it was a bad omen and not funny at all, but we chalked that up to those irrational superstitions to which Frank was surprisingly prone. But maybe he was right, or maybe his powers of prophecy were self-fulfilling, because one night, the boat sunk. Luckily only Yuri was on board. A life-long insomniac, he escaped easily. But he lost precious old belongings that Aunt Aki had given him, precious to both of us, the closest things to family heirlooms we had.

Among them were brittle old 78s, folk tunes and military marches from Japan's glory days. Yuri managed to retrieve a chipped recording of the "Kimigayo," the national anthem that had survived the journey from Japan, evacuation from Vancouver Island and the camps (escaping the eagle eye of the Custodian of Enemy Alien Property), and made it to Toronto. Yuri waited a month after he'd arrived from Amsterdam to call because, he said, he was used to me always calling him. As if I'd just divine when he was near—and often I suppose I did.

When he came over, we set the vinyl remnant on my old turntable and listened to the warble of dutifully ardent voices until the needle jumped off its broken edge. "They're all dead now," Yuri had said with what I took then for a wistful sadness like my own. But now I think it was wishful envy. I shivered with that old sensation from childhood, the sense of everything and everyone in my world coming to its end. I thought of my mother's fleeting carefree moods, her kimono sleeves and hair aflutter as she danced to "Strangers in the Night" when Frank worked late; I remembered birthday parties when Yuri and I could be together for hours at a time; I thought of my grandfather who loved purple irises, a man I barely knew who seemed too benign to be Frank's father.

Two and a half months after we'd buried Yuri's urn beside our grandfather, Frank took me to lunch at the top of the CN Tower. He'd live his entire life up among the clouds over water if he could, never having to touch ground except to leave his capacious footprint. He had left the family home on Fallingbrook and my mother and moved into the penthouse suite of one of his buildings on Queen's Quay. When we entered the restaurant, Frank lifted his brow to the maitre d' and we were promptly seated by the window that arced 360 degrees around us. I was dizzied by the view. My eyes followed the streets down to the snakes 'n' ladders curve of the expressway and couldn't help falling upon the lake.

"You looking for him, too?" Frank asked quietly.

The question that didn't require an answer, the barely lifted brow, Frank's more modest economy of movement honed over the years I hadn't seen him—or in the short months since Yuri's death—I noticed it now and it was unfamiliar. It lent him a dignity to which he'd long aspired in effect if not substance. I hadn't expected this change. It was less a mellowing due to age than a trimming of scraggly ends. I'd heard from my aunt Aki he'd been squiring some woman not much older than me, and she was Japanese again, but this time, straight from Nagoya—a JAL air hostess he'd charmed on a flight back from Tokyo. We both laughed with rue because Frank had met my mother when she'd served him on an Air Canada flight.

At that moment, oddly, I longed for the old Frank, the father of my child-hood: overweening, overbearing and utterly unknowing; always reaching too far too quickly, eager words forming on his lips before being uttered, even considered; a lick by the tongue in anxious lubrication, the subtle quiver of those lips as he verged on saying something, saying too much, giving himself away. The clown suit had long ago been put away, vanished up the sleeves. The clown would've thrust out his teeth at me, terrified me, chased me to the hysteria and horror from which I could never again be rescued by Yuri. I would've fled, run outside to the deck that ringed around us and finally looked onto the waters into which Yuri had silently plunged off the ferry to Ward's Island.

And then, reading my thoughts and getting them wrong, Frank said, "I still love it out there. He can't take that from me." I could only sit and watch my father's desperate, flitting eyes. The monkey Aunt Aki told me of, busily grasping for everything, believing that whatever escaped his grasp had been stolen from him.

I mimicked the quiet economy I'd observed in him. "He loved it too," I said. It was true: the water, the lake, the sea, it was what they both loved. The one thing they could share. Whereas I hated it: the dampness congesting my lungs, the black limitlessness of it day or night. You could never know what was lurking out there, waiting to swallow you up, Aunt Aki used to say.

My father's frantic eyes alighted on me and flared accusingly. "Don't look at me that way!" Then he leaned toward me, his hands prowling the table, the chair, his eyes growing evermore strange. "Don't you—" He stopped him-self. Then miraculously, those beautiful-ugly eyes disappeared under their lids, then reopened, and that voracious mouth trembled. "There's no one to blame." It was almost inaudible, yet he said it, as I knew he would. I knew he would excuse himself for every thing, big and small, for all that he inflicted on Yuri, on all of us, on this city. Just as my mother excused herself for marrying him and bringing me into his world.

I glanced up to find Frank crying. It was his clown face streaming, its formidable features collapsing. I'd never seen it before, not that I could remember. Not even at the funeral or the crematorium. "It's all right," he said. "There was nothing you could've done."

That I could've done? I?

I had to hear the question again and again in my head to apprehend its meaning. It was the tiniest minnow swimming upward through a murky sea; I couldn't catch it with my hands or see it with my eyes. But I followed it back to that night and the dark water frilled white that trailed at sharp angles behind us on the ferry I hadn't rode since I was a child. The sky was dark too, but splintered with orange all around the tower looming larger than life on the city skyline. The cold wind, so un-spring-like, tore my hair back; the water splashed my face again and again. I hated boat rides but Yuri had been desperate for me to come with him. He was beside me but hardly said a word, just thank you, close in my ear, and for a moment I was happier than I'd ever been to have him back. He'd left me for so long it seemed, and I remember that moment better than anything after.

Frank was still quietly weeping, but I couldn't turn away from the dark lake amid the too-bright sky and my last memory of Yuri. I had to get up. I did and Frank didn't stop me.

It took some time, in my confused state, to find the stairs. I knew they were there, that they existed, in case of fire, and for charity climbs. Yuri and I had been there the night the tower opened, when Frank was in his glory before the cameras, his arms around the young architect on one side and the engineer on the other, who'd fulfilled his vision. Yuri and I had huddled in the stairwell where together we unfolded a brochure and studied the diagram showing the tower's parts and the dimensions of what was proclaimed the tallest freestanding structure in the world. The steps were cold concrete, the handrail was cold steel; you could look down through a maze of landings. When I found the stairwell, it was all as it had been that night many years ago. I then held on to that handrail, stepping carefully, one step at a time, counting to keep myself from whirling headlong into the passageway down to the ground.

Packaging Parathas
Tasleem Thawar

89

Every morning, before school, Riyaz spent at least an hour packaging parathas. She had learned the process quickly, not long after moving to Toronto to live with her mother's eldest sister. Wipe the kitchen table. Lay out newspaper pages. Take care to keep aside those with coupons for Masi or crosswords for herself. The papers were from tenants in the building who handed them over to her every evening when their energy to read had been exhausted by their daily activities and television seemed a less ambitious pursuit.

The pages she collected were mostly from the *Toronto Sun* or the *Star*, and occasionally a *Metro* that had made it out of the confines of the TTC. Once a week her collection would be a bit heavier as everyone finished with the local community papers written in the Hindi and Urdu squiggles that she found incomprehensible. On the rare occasions when Aneel Uncle answered his door, he would give her his *Globe and Mail*, but mostly his wife would tell her that he left the paper at the office.

"No *Globe and Mail* today, Riyaz! Mr. Gilani has left his *Globe and Mail* at the office. He's a lawyer, you know, an important man! He reads the *Globe and Mail* everyday…no Sun-fun, Star-shmar for him…"

In fact, Aneel Uncle was a retired paralegal and his current office was usually the library on the corner or sometimes the coffee shop in the plaza. But Riyaz knocked on their door anyway because she liked to peek in to see what Mrs. Gilani was cooking so she could report back to Masi.

"Juby Auntie was making samosas in the OVEN!"

"This lady…she will never learn! Who will eat samosas from the oven? That's why even her husband likes to eat my cooking…"

Only a few newspapers made it to the garbage chute without ever having touched a single paratha. They belonged to people who Masi said might report them to the building management, or even the immigration people. Riyaz figured out quickly that these were people who had come to Canada a long, long time ago. Some were white, which Riyaz had expected, but the others, perplexingly, had somehow managed to cross over the Us&Them barrier, which separated those who felt they belonged in Canada from those who did not.

"I laid the newspapers, Masi!"

While brushing her teeth, she would watch through the bathroom door as Masi rolled out the dough and semi-fried the parathas, her heavy-set frame filling the kitchen. Her hands worked both quickly and gently as she evenly spaced them onto the newspapers. By evening they would be collected and frozen, to be thawed and thrown onto a frypan as needed by those who no longer had the time to roll circle after circle out of flour, oil, turmeric, fenugreek and chilies.

Most of the orders came from people who lived outside Flemingdon Park— sometimes they were even 905 numbers. Riyaz liked to imagine that they all lived in big houses, with three-car garages and maybe a swimming pool, and spent their days brunching on Masi's parathas with other 905-ers. But Aneel Uncle had many stories of couples like his son and daughter-in-law who worked endless days sandwiched by long commutes, only to return home with neither the time nor energy for paratha-making. Riyaz thought of it as the StandardofLiving-QualityofLife paradox: the achievement of one sometimes required the sacrifice of the other.

Wash face, back to kitchen table. Sip chai poured from a pot on the stove into a real china teacup. Check temperature of each paratha with palm of hand. Another sip.

• • •

Riyaz had known that moving from Dar es Salaam to live with Masi in Toronto would be the beginning of a new life in a new country, but living in a seniors' apartment building wasn't quite the life of excitement and opportunity that friends who had left Dar before her had promised. She was always hiding; Masi said that if too many people found out that Riyaz was staying with her, they could both be kicked out of the building.

But it was important to get a good education her mother had said, and so when she arrived here as a visitor two summers ago, she had known that she probably wouldn't be returning. She still missed her family and counted the days between their weekly phone calls, Masi dialing one week, and her Mum and Dad the other. She told them about her marks in school and her new friends, but not that she couldn't bring her friends home, or that her report cards had to go to an auntie's apartment in the building across the street. She knew that soon she would have to ask about what would happen next year; she wanted to apply to university in Canada, but tuition would be much more than her family or Masi could afford. She was avoiding asking the guidance counsellor for advice about loans, worried about what would happen if she knew that Riyaz wasn't supposed to be in the country.

Check parathas again. When cool to touch, flip over. Count out cellophane bags. Sort cooled parathas into piles of five, unless some were unusually small, and then six. Place in bags, keeping broken bits to a minimum.

Sometimes the ladies would complain to her about the size of the parathas.

"These are smaller today! I will only give you two-fifty for a packet."

"But there are six in those packets, Auntie, that's why they are smaller— you can count them!"

And the lady would hand her nine dollars for three packets and rush out, not wanting to spend too much time in the flat, lest her clothes start to smell of the parathas that she sooner or later would try to pass off as her own.

"Masi, these are done!"

"So fast? How can it be? Did you make sure they are cool? No one will buy if the bag is wet inside..."

"They're fine, Masi, bring more!"

♦ ♦ ♦

Throw out oily pages. Lay out new ones. Run behind curtain to find clothes for school. The bathroom had the only door in the flat—apart from the main door that opened out into the corridor. The remainder of the flat was separated by a curtain into a sleeping area with a double bed that she and Masi shared and a living space that contained both a plastic-covered sofa and a rectangular eating area denoted by a small rug. The wall-to-wall carpeting had been removed in the interest of easy clean-up and the floor was now covered in black-speckled white linoleum.

Rush back to new batch. Temperature check. Sip. Wait. Check again. Flip. Count bags. Sort. Wrap. Done.

"More, Masi!"

"Come and take from the pile!"

And, like this, before much of the world was awake, hundreds of parathas were cooled, sorted and packaged. Over just a few years, Masi's paratha orders had increased from just thirty or forty to sometimes more than two hundred a day, even though there were more and more ladies selling them from home. Some were taking care of young children, others were unable to work elsewhere because they had no immigration papers, and still others were hoping to supplement their fixed incomes. These ladies, like Masi, used the money to pay for daily trips to mosques and temples, or taxis home from the grocery store so they wouldn't have to walk or take the TTC. What they saved, they used to buy TVs and microwaves and presents for their grandchildren.

All this activity made the hallways in the building feel like marketplaces— each of the ladies was famous for a particular snack: either for being loyal to tradition—like Masi's masala parathas—or adapting to new times and diets—like Noorbanu-bai's samosas filled with chicken breast pieces instead of ground beef, and Kulsum Auntie's single-fried rather than double-fried meat cutlets. Many families would drive in rain or snow down the Don Valley Parkway and do weekend rounds of three or four different apartments and buildings to get the best of all the snacks for the week to come.

There were other income-generating activities as well, and Bilkis Auntie's was by far the most popular with ladies in the area. Riyaz was nervous when she first paid her a visit; she had been used to the salon in Dar es Salaam, where the endless gossip and laughter never failed to distract her from the pain of the hair being yanked from her legs. But salons were too expensive here, and it seemed that even the ladies who ordered parathas had their waxing done by someone like Bilkis Auntie. Her bed was stripped every morning, and each customer lay on towels with either their top or bottom halves exposed, flinching in time to the Velcro-like sound of the wax strips being removed. Riyaz had laughed when she noticed the photos of religious leaders that dotted the wall, amused that they were witness to the daily parade of half-naked ladies that passed them by.

Yes, it was fine for now, but Riyaz knew that come next year she would have to find a way to stay in the country. Her two years in Toronto would be a waste if she went home only to go to the University of Dar es Salaam. And no one had thought about what she would tell the authorities at the airport when they saw that she had overstayed her visa. She had asked Aneel Uncle about this once and he had laughed, "I doubt your packaging skills are going to be deemed essential to the Canadian economy anytime soon, Riyaz, so until the prime minister starts ordering parathas, we will have to think harder of what to do with you!"

Masi had never been illegal—she had arrived twenty years ago with her husband, who had been an electrician. It was easier then, everyone said. He had died of a heart attack just before Riyaz arrived, when Masi had managed to secure her flat in the seniors' building. Riyaz's arrival had been very lucky for both of them. Masi hadn't saved much, and was starting to feel very lonely when Riyaz had shown up. Moreover, Riyaz had turned out to be very good at paratha packaging, and Masi was planning to teach her how to make the dough and roll them out soon enough.

When the last batch of parathas was done, Riyaz would make her way to school, past the library and the Ontario Science Centre, where she had once had all of her hair stand on end as she touched a magic metal ball. Everyone had applauded and she felt like a star. There was nothing like that in Dar, she had thought. When she had told Aneel Uncle, he had laughed.

"Just wait Riyaz, everyone is eager to give a girl on a visitor's visa their applause, but just see if you will be able to get a job!" She had tried to escape down the hall, but his next comment followed her through the door into the flat. "Another second class citizen in a first class country..."

Things had gotten better since then, especially now that she had met Faria, who had moved from Nairobi a few years before Riyaz had arrived. She had taken Riyaz under her wing at school and invited her to eat lunch with her group of friends. They shared and traded the food they brought from home and, if it was nice out, they ate on the lawn, talking about homework and boys and long-term plans. She didn't think of her friends from Dar quite so much any more, but she missed their Sunday trips to Oyster Bay where they bought potato and cassava chips sliced and fried right there on the beach and served hot, drenched in tomato ketchup, chili and lemon. In Toronto, her weekly ritual was a walk to McDonald's with her classmates after school, where they ordered cheeseburgers and as many fries as they had the money for. This had been her first meal out when she arrived, laden with expectation, but she had been disappointed with the tasteless burgers and rubbery chicken. Nonetheless, her friends ensured that it became a weekly staple in her diet, and she felt happy to finally belong, one of a swarm of students who gravitated there as classes ended.

By the time she got home most of the parathas would be collected, and Masi would be cooking a ground beef curry with eggs or peas or potatoes, wiping her hands on her dress as she worked.

"What happened at school today, Riyaz?"

"Nothing, Masi—when will the kheema be ready?"

The smell of onion, garlic and garam masala made her mouth water, as she wiped down the kitchen table so she could lay out her books without staining them with bits of turmeric or splashes of oil that had gotten away. She was careful not to forget this ritual—she had been too embarrassed to hand in her first school assignment when she noticed in class that it was stained from the cutlets that had been lying on the table before she had started studying the previous night.

Sometimes she would tell Masi that she was going to study in the library, and when she got there, she would find Aneel Uncle sitting at a table surrounded by books and magazines. In exchange for one of Masi's parathas, he would tell her about what he had been reading and what had happened in the news that day. He had been looking out for her since she arrived, always briefing her on everything he thought she needed to know, from the location of the best dollar stores to the intricacies of Canadian politics. Over the past few weeks the news had mentioned illegal immigrants more often than usual, and Aneel Uncle had been reluctantly filling her in on the government's new plan for dealing with them. The last time she had met him, it had taken some persuading before he had told her about the other kids like her who had been rounded up in school and sent out of the country. It had scared her.

When she told Masi, she had waved her spatula in the air, angrier than Riyaz had ever seen.

"Who do they think they are—this Citizenship and Immigration Canada! You know why they are called that? Look at the spelling! See-eye-see!" she said angrily pointing to her eyeglasses. "They are watching everyone! We are all trying to have a good life, and they are trying to scare my Riyaz! C–I–C! See what it spells? Sick! They are sick, these people. Who will package their parathas if they kick you out? How will their precious workforce work twelve-hour days without our parathas? You tell me, Riyaz..." And then she went back to the kitchen to finish the kheema and it had turned out so spicy that Riyaz couldn't finish her dinner.

◆ ◆ ◆

Yesterday, when Riyaz had arrived home, she found Masi sitting on the sofa, a worried look on her face. Masi never sat down unless it was in front of a Hindi serial—if she wasn't cooking, then she was cleaning up, or doing laundry, or ironing, or something else that needed to be done.

"Masi? Are you okay?"

And Masi explained. She explained about a new shop that had opened close to the 905-ers. Where they sold parathas and cutlets and samosas at reasonable prices, and the quality was good, too. There had been talk about a shop like this opening for years now, and it seemed to have finally happened.

In the evening when Riyaz went to collect newspapers, she could feel the air thick with worry, the panic escaping in whispers through the cracks in the doors into the hall. Worried looks accompanied each "hello" as Riyaz completed her route, almost everyone shutting their doors quickly to get back to their conversations. Outside Noorbanu-bai's door Riyaz only had to lean in a little bit to hear her anxiety.

"What will happen now, Malik? Every day I am selling hundred samosas— if even half of our orders go, we will have to start saving money. See-pee-pee will never be enough."

"Arre…don't start worrying until the orders drop—who can resist my wife's famous samosas? No one, that's who! Tell me, what happened when that Thorncliffe Plaza shop opened? Nothing, that's what. How many customers did you lose? Not a single one…"

When Riyaz got home, she told Masi what she had overheard, hoping to reassure her. "Masi, maybe you don't have to worry—Malik Uncle says the new shop won't be a problem. That when the Thorncliffe Plaza shop opened everyone still had their orders…"

"He may be right, Riyaz, but already orders for tomorrow and the weekend are less than last week…what will we do if this new shop is really as good as they are saying? It will be so much closer for everyone to go there. How will we manage?"

"But not everyone lives in 905, Masi…don't worry, we have lots of orders from close by—in the building even! They will still order our parathas, and maybe we can start making other things too…"

"I don't know, Riyaz—We will have to wait to see…"

In the morning, things had already changed. Riyaz was at school early, because there had been fewer than a hundred parathas to pack, and she hadn't felt like staying in the flat with no work to do. When she left, Masi had turned on the television and had the phone by her side, hoping that someone would call to place an order.

School passed by quickly and when she got home Masi was hanging up the phone.

"An order, Masi?"

"Only a very small order, Riyaz."

"Oh. Didn't you make kheema?"

"Not today. We have cutlets and parathas and yoghurt. It should be enough."

In the evening when she went to collect the newspapers, the hushed panic had been replaced with nervous chatter as the ladies discussed the quality of the fare at the new shop. Each seemed to know someone who had tasted one of the new samosas, cutlets or parathas. Kulsum Auntie's nephew reported that the samosas were "big and meaty," while Noorbanu-bai's niece called them "cute and tiny." The parathas were called both "rich and buttery" and "light and flaky." In the end, no one could be sure that the reports were reliable or what the impact would be on their own orders.

When Riyaz got to Aneel Uncle's flat, she could see his grandchildren jumping on the sofa, and his son and daughter-in-law eating and laughing.

"Come in, Riyaz—it's Azam's birthday!"

She was happy to escape the anxious buzz in the hall, and put her newspapers down by the door. Samosas, cutlets, kababs and a big dish of chicken pilau lined the table, and there was a caramel pudding on the kitchen counter with a small card announcing "Happy 36th Birthday, Azam." Juby Auntie had folded coloured napkins into triangles, and handed her one with a samosa.

The samosa was light and crispy, filled with spicy minced lamb, and her chin was soon covered with the lemon she had squeezed into it. She took another.

"Auntie, these are good! Did you make them in the oven?"

"Don't be silly, Riyaz, Azam brought them from that wonderful new shop— did you hear? Such good food and so cheap! And not only samosas—Uncle says their parathas are too good! You should tell your Masi about it, Azam can bring for her to taste when he comes again..."

Riyaz held the half-eaten samosa in her hand, suddenly overcome. Already she had enjoyed one and a half samosas from the shop that she knew would change everything.

A plate of pilau and cutlets appeared in front of her. She accepted it half-heartedly, knowing that the longer she lingered, the more she could delay seeing Masi. She played with the children, talked to Azam about school, sang "Happy Birthday" and ate two pieces of cake. Eventually she could find no other reason to delay her return.

She picked up the newspapers that she had stacked by the door and left the warmth of the party, walking slowly down the hall, which somehow seemed cooler than it had earlier. She stopped outside her door, and listened to the muffled sound of the Hindi serial coming from the television inside the flat. Riyaz could picture Masi on their plastic-covered sofa with her feet up on the coffee table, waiting for her to come home so they could dial Dar es Salaam.

Correspondence
Fereshteh Molavi

99

Dear friend,

I am indeed thrilled I've finally found a friend I can write to, if not talk to. I hope that you don't mind if I number my letters to keep track of them easily. I trust this letter will find you well. I'm OK too. People say that life isn't perfect, but I have to admit that I'm really fine. I don't have any serious health problems. I have enough monthly income to live modestly. My new place is also fine—not as big as my house in Tehran, but enough space for a widower like me. It's a bachelor on the first floor of a lowrise building. My son says I'm lucky he's found such a nice affordable place where I can keep my privacy. He is absolutely right. Although my son and his wife were very nice with me while I lived with them, I didn't feel comfortable and happy. That's what he says, and he's right about that, too. He's got a good head on his shoulders and he always says the right things. That's why I didn't say no when he said, "Dad, you're alone in Tehran, sell the house and come to Toronto to live with us." My new place has a window that opens onto a narrow alley at the back of the building. A room with a window facing an alley, exactly like what I had in Tehran, when my son was a baby. He always wanted me to hold him up so that he could see the alley. "Isn't it what you wanted?" my son said on the day I moved in. He can read my mind. Across from my window one sees the backyard of a big house with a very old tree and a wooden fence. Opening the window, my daughter-in-law said, "Look, Dad, here is your garden, but you don't have to worry about collecting leaves." I nodded. She's such a smart woman! An old plane tree like this produces tons of leaves in autumn, I said approvingly. My son commented that it was a maple, not a plane tree, and my daughter-in-law smilingly reminded me that I was living in Toronto. You know, I'm very happy to have them refresh my memory. How about you? Do you have a good memory? Or do you too have someone to refresh your memory for your benefit? The family doctor, who my son took me to once, said that I had to work on my memory. That's how my son interpreted his words. I promised to do that. I asked my son to tell the doctor how I've always been proud of my memory. I still remember clearly how many nests of crows were in the plane tree beside my father's house. My son nodded and said a few words to the doctor, who nodded and smiled back at me. Canada has such understanding doctors, my daughter-in-law commented the other day. Now, every morning after my breakfast, I sit back on my armchair and think about my files. Believe it or not, it's never tough for me to remember where to find one file and where to find another. My letters of appreciation, of which only a few are framed and hang on the wall in front of me, prove that I was the best archivist in Tehran's birth registry. The one that I received in my first year of service has golden decorations in the margins. Moreover, my clients were happy when they noticed that I recalled details about them and their families. "Hey, man, you're lucky to be the father of seven daughters—don't tell me you're here for the eighth one!" Or, "My friend, I'm so sorry you lost a baby son again." Or, "Look, old man, are you going to kill your wife with non-stop babies?" Well, I didn't make a big effort. You know, I just did my job and my brain did its job. That's it. How about you? Do you have a rewarding job too? Does your boss appreciate your faithful work? I don't expect you to write me long letters. We're both busy, just like other people. It's nice, though, to have a line once in a while from a dear friend like you.

Yours,
A.

Dear friend,

Interestingly, you are as well organized and punctual as me. That's why I receive your letter every other Monday. Certainly, you get my letter on time, too. You're so important to me that, on the appointed day, I sacrifice my morning memory exercise and go out after breakfast to mail my letter to you. Such has been my routine since we started to correspond. Sometimes, on my way back, I get off the bus one stop ahead to have tea in a coffee shop always full of elderly men discussing world affairs or playing backgammon. Well, my son thinks that it's good for me to socialize with my peers. They are immigrants, too, so you shouldn't be ashamed of your broken English. That's what he says. Obviously, he has no idea of the time the Allies soldiers were hanging around the streets in Tehran. Who was ashamed then? A school boy like me who spoke French fluently, or those tall lads who couldn't understand Farsi or French? This aside, what do I have to say to these talkative old folks who think they know how to solve the world's problems? Occasionally, I play backgammon with a quiet Greek man who never joins the others' political discussion. Otherwise, we might have argued about our ancestors' wars. To make my son happy, I've told him about this Greek guy. You can practice English with him, my son says. Do we need English to play backgammon with Greeks or to fight with them? What about grocery shopping? my daughter-in-law once asked. I certainly don't like to disagree with her, because she's really nice. That's why I didn't say no when she encouraged me to go to an evening dance class for elderly people. But you know how these old women are. To know your life story doesn't make them happy enough. They want to know the whole history of your tribe. And when you talk about history, obviously you step on their toes in a way that no apologies can make up for. You become ashamed. My daughter-in-law agreed with me and gave up the idea of the dance class. What about you? Do you have to go to any classes? "No matter how old you are, it's wonderful to go to classes, either to learn something useful or just for the fun of it," she used to tell me when I was living with them. Certainly, I have no doubt about things like this. You should know that I'm not fanatically trendy; I simply want to avoid stress. Tell me, honestly, isn't it stressful to be a gentleman? Or worse than that, to face nonstop challenges to show that you're up to date? Anyway, you surely know what I mean. That's why we are very willing to communicate with each other. You may know that nobody writes me, other than you. How about you? Do you have any relatives or friends to write you? Are you a widower like me? I wonder if I already told you about the day of my wife's funeral. A bright winter day, exactly like today, the sun in the sky, the snow on the earth, and the house was as crowded as if all the people who she had ever met were there. The week after, I found myself as alone as Adam was in Paradise. To tell the truth, I was not unhappy at all. The only problem was that I didn't know what to do. When my wife was alive, she assigned me duties, either outside, like shopping, or inside, like changing light bulbs. I found myself a man without duties, as if she had taken along all the errands with her into the underground. Such a considerate woman she was! There are so many things one can do. That's what they say—I mean my son and his wife. Of course, there are so many things to do. But does a wise man bother himself doing so many things? Surely you would say no, for you are a wise man too. Anyway, I'd better end this letter now. You'll forgive me for being so wordy.

Looking forward to hearing from you soon.

Yours,
A.

LETTER #27

Dear friend,

I hope this letter will reach you on time and find you well. In fact, I should have written you yesterday, but I didn't. You don't think that it happened because of my memory is dysfunctional, do you? For some reason I was simply absent-minded. What did I do? Well, probably, the same things I do every day. For sure, I had breakfast because I don't remember being hungry before lunch. Maybe I had my lunch in the morning and my breakfast at noon. I have to confess that this happens sometimes. To me it's not a big deal, despite the fact that my son takes it as a serious proof of my decline. Anyway, in the evening, I watched TV in my own style, which means with the mute button on. If my daughter-in-law found out that I watch TV but I don't listen to it, she would blame me for not taking this opportunity to improve my English. You don't think like her, do you? Please, don't ask me which channel, or which program, or what time. I don't pay attention to things like these. My son insists on convincing me that I should work on my short-term memory. He says that I can't remember what I've just done or seen or heard. I don't argue about things like this, but I tell you he is wrong. What problems do I have now? Well, anybody may forget what he is supposed to do now or where he put his key or which bus stop he should get off at. These are all trivialities. Anyway, what's up in your world? Nothing special? Are you bored? This is how I easily amuse myself: I collect all flyers, catalogues, brochures and free newspapers. I categorize and file them in the used binders I buy at garage sales or the Salvation Army shops. I tag binders and shelve them beside my books on the book case. This is something, though my son and his wife think it is a useless hobby. My policy is not to argue with them. Otherwise I could prove to them that it's no more futile than all the other hobbies. Needless to say, one may do all the things people do to amuse themselves, like reading bestsellers, listening to the news, watching soap operas, etc., etc. But tell me, do we have to follow others? Sometimes, I put my armchair close to the window and look out. But despite what my daughter-in-law thought, I don't enjoy watching my neighbour's garden. This old tree hardly ever attracts crows. It might be because crows like Tehran more than Toronto and planes more than maples. No wonder if such is the case. So, why do I sit next to the window? Well, occasionally I like spying on the squirrels running up and down the trunk or jumping from a branch to another, though they are not as amusing as the stray cats parading day and night in all the alleys and streets of Tehran. What I enjoy most is staring at a point, each time a different point, either in midst of the foliage, or on the pointed tops of picket fences, or at the edge of one of two big trash bins, and letting my mind go wherever it wants to. Definitely you won't ask me what's the use of it, as they would if they noticed me sitting by the window for hours. They think whatever I do is useless. Well, it might be true, though I doubt what they do is useful either. You know what I mean, don't you? You may say that it's a matter of different generations. I would say it's a matter of...anyway, let's change the subject; I forget the word I meant. Thank God you don't have such problems with your children. But tell me if you have any children at all. Please pardon my ignorance. It's not that I'm not concerned about you.

Looking forward to hearing from you soon.

Yours,
A.

P.S.:
My son came by this past Monday to bring the cheque for the landlord. As it happened, he ran into the mailman in the lobby and took your letter from him. He was surprised that I had a letter from a Toronto friend.

Dear friend,

I'm hoping to find a way to get out and mail this letter to you. You should know that they keep a close watch on me. Can you imagine that one day your son forbids you to go out? He is not alone; his wife is his accomplice. They've threatened me to send me to a nursing home. Shame on them! Don't tell me to be patient with them. How can I ignore their malicious behaviour? They say they do this for my own good. Is it good for me to stop communicating with you? Do I have any friend other than you? My son suspects your letters just because they're sent from Toronto. I wish you were in Tehran. But then, how could I correspond with you? Moreover, I don't remember if I ever heard from you when I lived in Tehran. Maybe it was my wife's fault that she never left me without errands after my retirement. I know it's not good to badmouth a former wife, but I can't keep my mouth shut while I see that her son and her daughter-in-law are intriguing against me. Yesterday, no, the day before yesterday, I don't remember if it was in the morning or in the afternoon, anyway, when I was leaving home, the superintendent barred my way and gave me a piece of paper with a note in Farsi saying, "Dad, if you need to buy anything or mail a letter, please call me. I'm worried in case you get lost. Love, your son." Can you believe it? As if I'm a kid, not knowing what to do or where to go. Isn't it insulting? What does the guy, the superintendent, think about me? Thank God, he doesn't know Farsi. You ask me what I did? Well, I smiled and nodded and thanked him. In order not to raise more suspicions, I didn't leave the building. Yet my daughter-in-law called me later and asked if I needed anything. Then when I was in bed, my son called and said he just wanted to be sure that I was OK. How nice they are! They poke their nose into my life and claim they care about me. In fact, they are obsessed with our letters. They can't stand that I have a relationship with someone other than them. Remember how many times I wrote about their insistence on my socializing with others? Dad, you should be more outgoing! Dad, isn't there any nice woman in your ESL class? Dad, it's not bad to have a drink and chat with friends. Well, now you see how hypocritical they are. The first time he noticed I had a letter from you, he said, "Very good, so you have a pen pal friend now, but why don't you meet each other?" How did he know that we hadn't met each other? He was suspicious from the very first moment. I may forget my address, or my phone number, but I'm sure that I never ever said anything indicating we hadn't met each other. Honestly, I doubt we hadn't. I mean not in Toronto, or maybe even not in Tehran as far as I can remember. But in the very past, perhaps, somewhere I don't recall, I guess I met you. Don't you think so? And then we lost track of each other. I, myself, got swamped—with duties and errands, Well, that's life. I'm happy I found you again. This time, I'm not going to lose you. I'm not saying that I regret I was a good employee or a good family man. One may say that I was this and that by nature. What I regret is that I didn't have any secret for myself. You know what I mean. I'm sure you value our secret too. No matter how my memory works, we write letters and we mail them. I take enough precautions. What else do they want me to do? By living on my own I'm proving to them I'm not crazy or incapable of taking care of myself. Why should I live in a nursing home? I don't deny that sometime I make mistakes. However, it has nothing to do with my intelligence. Yesterday, or the day before yesterday, I had no plan to go out to mail the letter. I did that to cheat them. Moreover, on my last phone conversation with my son, I said to him, "One would have to be an idiot to write to oneself. You don't think your father's an idiot, do you?" What did he say? Well, he believed me. Now it's time for you, my dear friend, to believe that I will mail this letter to you soon, in good time. Don't ask me how! I'll tell you in my next letter, if I don't forget.

Yours,

A.

Plan to Make Do

Michele Chai

109

I) GETTING BY

—"Ow…yo, that *hurt*."

A young woman jams her elbow into my chest shoving me out of her space. Her distracted exit from a department store propels her small pod of friends askew. My chest hurts, not in a call-the-ambulance kind of way but in a startled unexpected physical-contact-with-a-stranger kind of way. People simply don't get that close, that fast, unless they're force-fed onto public transport during rush hour and get stuck with a driver whose foot is as heavy on the gas as it is on the brake.

My squeak of protest enlists her friends, who now want to pick a fight— with me.

I get shoved. I know better than to shove back.

"Yuh must be making joke.

"Yuh want tuh fight me, after yuh almost knock mih ass down?

"But cross my stars. Chile, don't let me go an' find yuh mudder," my finger wagging in the air like dragonfly wings.

But that would be small island talk. And I would have to look like a mother to make any such threat. A fifteen-year-old lost his life last week over a bus ticket. Instead I yell, "Why is it everyone is so ready to fight?"

"Ready, ready, allyer ready fuh a fight?"—"Come lemme see yuh. Lemme see yuh!"

I am unable to take back the "fuck you" that leaks out of my mouth on the trail of their combined threat to mash me up.

It is cold and grey and rainy and Saturday. My clothes are damp and I feel miserable. I rearm myself. And with my ball cap pulled low, brim arching my eyes, I stride through the newly renovated one-stop-shop of Gerrard Square. There is an uneasy swell of anticipation in the pit of my stomach. I readjust my old-school DJ headphones with the volume turned to an almost deafening pitch and try to find sanctuary as I muffle out the frenetic sounds of weekend shoppers. The deep bass of "Amnesty" draws my fear away and, like intuitive automation, I automatically erect blinders as well. I focus on the list in my pocket as long as my arm.

"We want some amnesty. Put down the guns in my country...we want some amnesty..."

II) GETTING THERE

I rarely read when I travel through this city. I don't sleep anymore either. Since my school days there doesn't seem to be a long enough route to pull me weary against the cool metal edge of a window section. An alertness, to which I have not grown accustomed, shrouds my daily commute. These days the city feels different—there is a tightness in unexplained movement(s), a certain kind of irritation or suspicion about anyone doing anything with the potential to jar another person from the safety of their imaginary bubble.

On most days I take the same route at the same time with pretty much the same people. There are the drivers who never say good morning and the ones who are elated whenever anyone says thank you. Today, a man bound tight in his navy blue suit, oblong tie and perfectly creased trousers—stands in the middle recess of the 501 Queen East. He exits at Victoria Street gripping his briefcase tightly in one hand and his take-away coffee in the other. His voice is tense as he negotiates with someone on the other end of his wireless headset in a lingo I don't get.

As the streetcar judders west, the just-before-Osgoode-stop-lawyer—forever running late—is walking as he scans his briefs, hardly lifting his gaze from the page. On this morning, like most others, I smile and say good morning into his blank stare. I muse at how easy it would be to fall seamlessly into big-city monotone anonymity and simply go about my day ignoring the rest of the world because I'm either too busy or too tired or just numb.

Occasionally someone responds the way I (still) expect them to—with an acknowledgement, some small recognition of my humanity, an indication of theirs. It is usually someone older, someone brown, someone whose work-weary life lines their palms and shoulders and face—or someone who like me, may have reluctantly acclimatized themselves to moving through this bustling city invisible.

I close my eyes and the image of a dusty hot street in Port of Spain swims into focus. I see a precocious girl-child trying to make eye contact with passersby—an imitation of what she sees grown people do. With a smile or a nod she acknowledges neighbours and strangers alike. She feels connection and community. She knows she belongs. I can't help but smile at my city with its small pockets of community about—Kensington Market, Little India, weekday afternoons in Chinatown. But like a petulant child I want more than pockets of belonging from my city. I want to feel again like I always belong. I want to know that people care, that they see me, that we see each other.

A jolt from the streetcar drags me into the reality of having reached my stop. I hustle out of my seat and push past the closing doors to stumble out into the light of the street. A yellow Nissan Xterra is already lurching past the streetcar doors to charge the amber light. I gasp as I thrust my hand out, expelling an exasperated "Yo!" as the vehicle screeches to a halt to reluctantly let me by. My heart pounds in my head.

I wobble down the dingy stairs leading to the bowels of the city's subway system.

III) GETTING HERE

As the edge of my seat meets my back, I am aware that this is the first time I've sat still all day. I throw my head back in quiet appreciation of having made it through yet another day. There is a woman surrounded by nondescript white plastic shopping bags—her head resting lightly against the partition glass between her seat and the doors. A woman cradling a child on her lap argues with someone on the phone. I assume it is her lover as she begins to counter what may be accusations about where they were all day and with whom. A group of youth with skateboards and rainbow-tagged backpacks on the floor are all plugged into their individual mp3 players, while one guy sends a text message on his phone. They don't talk or make eye contact and I can't even be sure they are together, but I merge the group by my perception of their shared interest.

I am sitting here uncomfortable in my longing. My head is heavy and my eyes loose like a box of pushpins ready to cascade off the edge of a desk. It's been too long since I've seen my lover. My skin is tight with anticipation as I crave her length. I'd rather be travelling a longer distance to see her than on this dismal train heading to my empty apartment. I unzip my bag and reach for my journal: an ordinary, wire-bound, hardcover sketchbook fraying at the edges from overuse. I want to finish the poem I started for her and as I finger the book's wire bend that usually houses a pen I remember I don't have one. I am thoughtful as I reread my hastily scribbled lines of verse.

Holding pattern

Too often pieces from my past come to me like fireflies in the distance—
distorted images flickering into focus that swiftly float away

I tug at the details through years of hazy drunkenness
hoping to arrive at the truth
and wonder what might have been different if the pain
of immigration and coming out did not push me
to caress the long cool necks of cheap beer and one night stands

Does it matter if I can't remember their names?
Or that I say I'm not a recovering alcoholic
because I didn't go through a twelve-step program?

I'm not really sure what matters
But what I do know is that I made it though my teens and twenties
with too many scars to name
And with self-inflicted wounds and broken bones I fold into you
because you are not too terrified of my leaky cobwebs
to hold me close…

The train eases to a screechy lazy halt to avoid scattering weary commuters and I rise to exit on my trying-to-slow-down-evening home. I smile wide when I notice your pens—about four blue ones, a red and a black pen. So I say to you "where were you when I needed a pen this morning?" You are startled. You're not sure you hear me because you have probably never heard the voice of a fellow passenger addressing you on that exhausting journey home before. I may as well have stepped into the curve of your chest and placed my arm around your shoulders, because you take a deliberate step back. I repeat myself, then babble that "I noticed your pens, the ones in the mesh outer pocket of your backpack—and it reminded me that I needed one this morning, so, where were you when I needed a pen this morning?" You are clenching your jaw—a furrowed, questioning glance highlights your five o'clock shadow greying in the dimly lit subway car. My face is a jumble of amusement and disappointment as I edge out the door. As the train begins to pull away I peer over my shoulder to see you looking at me, still, but this time it is you wearing an amused smile. I saunter up the escalators and head into the chill of the night.

I reach inside and there's a little red light on my phone. Most evenings it's an eyebrow-raising *"yuh* mean no body *eh* call here?" green light that makes me wistful, but this evening I am distracted by the weight of my day.

As the door slides shut behind me, I try to shake the wind off my back. I shed layer after layer in an attempt to escape its icy grip. It sticks to my bones the way tar clings to the soles of my feet on a post-storm stroll along the beach. I wish the wind here were more like island wind. In Trinidad, at least the wind is a breeze and that breeze bathes you into believing you belong. The wind here is hard and harsh and a reminder that this is not a belonging kind of place. It is just a getting-by kind of place. As pointless as it is, I continue to try to peel the wind off. But just like tar, it will stay stuck until it is good and ready.

On days like today, by the time I reach home, my mind is quiet in a noisy kind of way.

IV) GETTING HOME

The humidity hits me square as I step out the door of the plane and descend onto the tarmac. There are few places left in the world where a body can move heel to hot pitch en route to immigration. I revel in this small freedom—chin tilted toward blue sky, eyes sun-blasted shut. This is familiar—the smell, the feel of the island on my skin. This is real—heat rising off the road after rain, warm, intoxicating pulling me with my Trinidad passport in hand like an exhausted child to her bed. I am comforted by this welcome. I enter as a local even though I have not set foot on island soil in over five years. Foreign local. Everyone can tell by my clothes that I don't live on the island. When my words tumble out of my mouth I am told that I sound like I never left.

I am hardly off the plane and I begin peeling back the layers so my sweat can run freely. Each hair pasted curly against the length and breadth of me. I am wildly happy in the hot, humid air. This is the only place in the world I can be sticky and wet and wear a smile on my face all at the same time. My body aches to lie exposed, to taste the rain, the sun, to feel the caress of salted air on my skin. I am here to find myself, to lose my bearings, to experience anew. I am here to steal and stash memories for my return to the icebox. I am here to collect a few pieces of the puzzle that is me begun in this place. I am also here to say goodbye to my grandfather. I wonder what has changed since I was here last. Change I can deal with. It's the things that stay the same that make me ache.

In my dream a woman speaks to me in a language I cannot place—in a place that feels familiar. So familiar that paying attention to detail doesn't matter. Doesn't cross my mind. I know that tomorrow, in five minutes or five hours, that face will still be here. She is showing me a map, the details of my history. Her soft fingers turn to bone as she traces the distance between China and the Caribbean Sea. I nod as if I understand but I don't quite get it and I know that none of the information she is giving me I will retain. She gestures to my nine-year-old self, huddled in grief on a bench in a schoolyard.

I startle awake, sleep stuck wearily against my cheek. I am clutching a photograph of my grandmother.

Memories are unreliable, imperfect—like dreams, jagged and broken...

I struggle to pull the sleep from my eyes. Heavy curtains against the reality of another day ahead. Yes. I am still here. And—it is still cold outside. On mornings like these I just want to be home or somewhere else but here. I want to pull the sunlight from my eyes as I roll wearily around my bed. I want to start the day feeling like I belong somewhere. I sigh and wonder where that place would be. What would it smell like, sound like, feel like? Would I recognize it? I surface hoping wherever it is, it smells like my bed and my fingers waxy with you and the nape of your neck when I wake. My phone rings and it is you—my evening-dusted, husky-throated lover. I breathe you in—drag you under with me as I pull the covers over my head. "Tell me again WHY IT IS I have to get up?" My first smile of the day begins to stretch groggily across my face.

Memories are unreliable, imperfect—just like yesterday and all the days before them.

V) GOING HOME

She is late. I am standing alone, cigarette hanging lazily from my lips, wait-ing. Everyone has scattered. With bags in hand, smiles on cheeks, shooting stories of their journeys so fast heads nod like a chorus line of broken jack-in-the-boxes. They are all heading to places that are familiar to them. Places many take for granted. There was a place like that for me once. But I've been gone so long that the beads of my life that cling to that place are quickly becoming symbolic rather than real in time or memory.

When I left Toronto, the weather was mid-December cool. My jacket and jeans are now bundled into my knapsack. I am standing against a railing with the sun on my skin and I am happy to be home. I am home, although I have never been to this place. I am waiting for my lover, whom I barely know in flesh time, to meet me. When we finally embrace, it is clear that our attempt to bridge the miles between us is what makes this moment familiar. I close my eyes eager to make the memory of this second first-meeting last.

But everything falls into and out of place in one silly second. It is as if I've lived a lifetime here, and the nostalgia I feel floors me.

A year prior I was in a similar place. Waiting for someone to pick me up from Piarco International Airport. At the time I was mildly amused that I was not sure who that would be. Anyone who would usually greet me would likely be preparing funeral arrangements. So there I was standing in Trinidad's brand new airport—lost—in a place where memories are burned into my bones. As people scattered by taxi, maxi taxi and private car I tried to remember if I told anyone exactly when I was coming. It was unusual for me to be guessing how much a taxi fare home would be. I remember looking at the phone and thinking *"What de ass?"* There wasn't a slot for coins. I was going to have to find somewhere to buy a card that will work in a phone I didn't know how to use. What I really wanted was a hot loaded doubles—my father's stop-by-the-roadside ritual when leaving the old Piarco. I felt trapped by both the newness and the familiarity of being home.

My memories. Are they just stories I've made up about my childhood? Why is it that who I understand myself to be now dangles on something as intangible as time physically spent in a place?

The last time I moved, I noticed that the process of packing and unpacking —deciding what stays and what goes, particularly because this included a dissolution of shared items—was a major source of stress. I realized that every time I move I get better at letting go, at holding on and at transition. I am a bundle of contradictions. My memories of home are like this. I am in constant negotiation over the right to claim somewhere as my own. I wonder if my life would be simpler if home were just one place. One place to build memories and bury loved ones. I decide it might be simpler but it wouldn't be real for someone like me. There are too many of us scattered across continents having left people and pieces of ourselves in places we are both eager to return to and eager to forget. I wonder when home began to be and mean so many different things at so many different times.

I pick up the phone to quiet the little red light inviting me to retrieve my messages. It is my mother and my lover, both on different continents, asking me to phone home. As the rhythm of their voices soothes me, the winter wind lifts off my back.

Poems
Evan Placey

118

MATTHEW GOLDMAN AT SUNDAY BRUNCH
AT KIVA'S RESTAURANT

Sugar, Stephen, Pass the Sugar, sweet eyes stare at me, my name is Matthew, Zelda is
shoving ten dollars into my hand so Melvin won't see, lox flop onto the table top
and her dyed-blond locks are falling out, don't know what she's going on about, it's
Yiddish or Hungarian, and Stanley is dozing, cream cheese spit bubbling at his
lips, Zadie's kissing Sarah, shaking salt on his matzah balls and dandruff is snowing
into my orange juice, reach for my coffee but Bubbie is bringing it to her hot pink
lips, she sips, *who's your shiksa?* she's not mine, she's Stephen's and she's Jewish, and
Stephen laughs, *where's your girlfriend?* he's a homo, Estelle, now, *no, skim please,*
homo, *what?* feygalah, *who wants rugalah?* and Louis is snoring, waitress pouring
more murky syrup into his mug, and drugs, so many drugs, orange and yellow,
teeth, see, me, and brie on rye and Louis's eyes half open dreaming of gefilte fish or
gas showers, my jacket's going on, and Baruch Atah, Louis awake, Adonai, though
we've eaten, bobbing along to the song, slip past fast as I can but don't miss the
kiss from Zelda, with five more dollars in my hand, duck out and the stamped kiss
begins to melt in the wet and freeze, Amen.

BRITISH BOY/CANADIAN BOY

A blown kiss floats above the ocean, lingers
        dreamt, a thumbprint stamped
from nectarines with fuzz of peach and stubble of
        face, lobe of ear, grazed,
bitten gently.
The nectar drips down
        soft neck of smoke, sweat, sweet
smell of Indian summer, legs and twigs entwined, not tangled.
        Burning blue and brown
eyes look away, the music stops but doesn't.
And he and he fuck
And he and he make love
And he and he coffee through the rain walk that pours
        wine on his t-shirt of flowers.

A smiling text, he cries of passion, of
pain. A morning stir,
        a phone on the pillow, murmurs and   whispers of
sleep, ruffled hair, brush
        of sex.
Fingers touch and trace
        the outline of feet, fear, feel
of trousers and/or pants and/or underwear spilled on the
floor, a flood of photographs, stains.
And he and he scream
And he and he lick sores
And he and he wade through letters,
write, teach, finger the spine of the book back, tongues.

And he and he hold hands above the ocean.
Breathing under the water.

MARGIN

I.

Ten children, nervous squawking chickens
peer up at the greasy limp hair and sweat-stained dark clothing
black magic-marker make-up that is their counsellor
for the next two weeks.
Nine checkmarks,
one worried face.
You said your name was Jennifer?
Nod, nod.

The name on the list resembles Jennifer like a monkey resembles a dog.

Pointing to the mishmash,
Goth face asks the hopeful eyes:
Is this your Chinese name?

Slits of anger. *I'm Korean.*

II.

So I'm like, I didn't say that y'know?
If Sherri's a lying slut that's her probs yo
Cause it's not my fault y'know?
I never said I'd drive her.
You sure you didn't promise when you were wasted?
Don't be gay. I'd remember.

III.

Écoutez. Et répétez s'il-vous-plaît.
Listen. And repeat after me.
Bonjour, je m'appelle François.
Bonjure, je maple france.
Elle s'appelle Chantelle.
El apple chant.
Il aime manger les crêpes.
Eel am monjay crep.
Nous voulons fumer.
*Nous vool on…if they'd just separate already we wouldn't be forced
to take this class.*

IV.

I promise I didn't promise I'd go
You know what that bitch is like, y'know?
I never was gonna go
Know what I mean, man.
I guess so. Yeah.
You guess so? You can be such a faggot sometimes.

V.

Warm Saturday afternoon, not a day
for colour-blind spectators,
for he says it had just turned yellow
and she says the light was red
and now his front black bumper is showing lines of silver from under
and her green back bumper has scars of black.
You stopped short, lady, says he.
It was a red, says she.
This is why I hate fucking Chinese people, they don't know how to drive, he says.
Maybe if your black music wasn't so loud, you'd have seen the red, she says.

VI.

Ten women, a chorus
line perfectly in synch, perfectly
still,   stripped of shoes and clothing, stamped
on the arm, underside, below the elbow
with matching arm tattoos.
The second from the left is shot, the fourth from the right is
shot.

The fence glimmers in the rising sun.

VII.

In the mirror a pensive face.
Creased forehead, engraved,
            a history of anger.
Well-watered eyes, heavy with strain,
bags padded with the strength of healed wounds.
I pick at the dried blood and I
ask the mirror, and
I ask you:

find the line.

Poems
Ian Malczewski

125

january — ward's island beach

yes, this places still exists in winter,
although reduced ferry service and
a wind that rattles the bones
of the skeletal trees lining the beach
certainly make it less accessible.

and the sand is coarse and hard—
the weight of too many ghosts
has compressed it and the ice has cooled
summer's too-hot-to-stand-in dreams.

but the pole we took turns throwing
stones at still stretches from the sand
and the spot we drifted to about twenty metres out
still glistens from the sun
and the memory of that moment.

if i close my ears and pull my toque over my eyes.
i can see us running around me:

i'm wearing my red bathing suit,
you're half-wearing your birthday suit
and we're smiling and running,
kicking sand in the face of my future self.

your friends are with us, too:
e.e., theodore and the polish
woman whose name we could never pronounce,
though she pronounced ours just fine.

i'd take their books from
the pocket where i've kept them,
but it's too cold to turn the pages
and, anyway, they're somewhat
surly in cooler weather.

still, their muffled speech somehow makes
its way to my ears, and while the air freezes some words,
most of them are clear if i listen just right, and put their verse
in your voice.

you might ask me (and in fairness)
how these words could be true if
the other ones, the ones i dare
not repeat, implicitly pursue.

and your friends and our ghosts
will freeze and cock their heads,
waiting for the answer that's brought
me this far, to this perfect beach
iced over in the dead of winter:

"i'm in the wrong place at the wrong
time. i follow the timing of the ferries, i set
my watch by the boatman, not he
by mine. it's that intersection of sand
and water, where the grains of me
are pulled into the infinite of you. it's these
ghosts that rattle on my flesh, it's their
smiles, incapable yet full of foreknowledge.
it's me missing that pole with the first
few throws, not expecting the
'ding!' of solemn, perfect connection.
it's the wall of words i throw up to
deflect something we both know. it's
skipping stones on the surface over
the abyss of us, but not following them below.
it's hoping some place in the sand that marks where we sat
remembers the shape of our bodies even if they never go back."

"it's none of those things,"
you say, and your hands slide
the toque from my head
and a rare winter heat wave
ripples across the island
where in our moments most
isolated and free
we imagined a future without this winter,
this forgotten, frozen beach
occupied only by me.

vigilante
>—posted on a window: yonge and gould

this cold concrete staunches heat from me
but it pulled worse from you:

when dark, impenetrable
clouds fell from the sky,
street and sidewalk
dimmed and thunder and lightning
tore the earth apart between us.
invisible hands screamed out and pulled
you into swirling nothing.
when the clouds dissipated—
sucked underground through ventilation grates
and cracks in the pavement
and rat holes down polluted alleys—
screams and coughing and the slick syrup
of your life glinted fading light to my
half-blind eyes. the sparkle of tears sprinkling
your bed looked like a sea of candles. they
looked like your shrine.

i lay on the ground and felt something
lift from the earth. the empty
inverted cap between my legs
shuddered.

now, weeks later, the crowds have returned and
your shrine has coagulated and stuck to the pavement.
i melted together some wax to seal this letter
before the city announced the candles and flowers were
a tripping hazard.

god i hate the sidewalks of this place and the street cleaners that rumble by and
spin water and dirt into my face. the drunken short-skirted gaggles of teenage girls
sneering at my torn shirt.

into hot wax i stamp
my thumbprint and scrawl two words
on an envelope made out of the front page of the paper
showing your smiling face, framed by the
arches of your blond hair.
around the corner
is mr. mackenzie's printing press, though
the *colonial advocate* is long gone—
no one stirs up the masses to
march down yonge street anymore.

the heart of the city indeed:
burst, heart, burst!

dear [unintelligible]:

tonight i take up arms and kiss the pavement—
insomnia pushes me through cracks and hollows.
let those dark clouds drop from the sky
let one more arm reach out to snuff one more life
let me pump cold vengeance
into that typhoon of void, let me pull on those arms,
yank the cowl of the executioner clear off his head
to stare in his eyes
wild animal fear
watering from the stench of my
un-bathed body.

to sink these blades past
the iris
to pour blind blood across
yonge street
to bellow your name
in its gouged face
and then disappear
on broken, dirty feet.

apology

so the subway smells like
stale tim hortons coffee
double doubles spilling
over stained winter mittens
and tarnishing orange-gold
floors like slush.

and just beneath that is the
rank stench of morning breath—
not just one person's—

a whole city's worth of
tartar and plaque sticking to the
walls of the train. my stomach
turns at the
thick green haze of
coffee and breath floating between
shampoo and debt counselling
advertisements.

this briefcase in my hand
could be carrying the complete
works of geoffrey chaucer,
although that isn't quite right.
my plastic arm creaks
as i attempt the ballet of
passing brief case to left hand
while placing right hand on the pole,
an epic struggle that earns
few sympathetic glances

an announcement crackles that
i can't quite hear, although
what sense does one ever make
of the phantom shouting
numbers over our heads?
we trust that the words
five oh six bathurst
five oh six please call
mean that somebody, somewhere
is making sure we get to
where we're going.

when the doors chime open
the putrid air shimmers
through the cold of the outside.
it's like watching an
exorcism.

in fantasies
someone pushes the emergency strip.

if this suit wasn't so tight
and this briefcase so heavy
i wouldn't be scratching these words on the inside
of subway doors on the way home every day:

i'm sorry i failed to change the world.

Amah
Devyani Saltzman

I found her in literature only once, hiding in Salman Rushdie's short-story *The Courter.* London, 1962, an Indian nanny walking down a street in Kensington with the edge of her "red-hemmed white sari" in hand. Amah did the same as she cut through the pedestrian pathway at the end of our street, making a beeline for the 7-Eleven. But unlike Rushdie's Kensington ayah, Amah never met and fell in love with the Eastern European hall porter of her employer's building. She never had liaisons that involved a shared love of chess.

Amah came to Canada when I was eight weeks old. I was told that her husband beat her and drank, although I never met him and she never talked about the beatings. Romantic love was of no interest to her, and whenever she saw a couple kissing on television and in the movies she'd say "chee chee" in disgust and turn away. She arrived in our lives through the recommendation of an aunt in Delhi. Her previous charges had been the children of diplomats, although I couldn't imagine Amah rotating through the three-year cycle of embassy employees. All we knew was that she had come from a village outside Bangalore in the south Indian state of Karnataka. She was illiterate, the mother of five daughters, and didn't know her own age.

Amah would fly back to Toronto with my parents in January 1980. Canada required a work permit and a passport at that time, neither of which she had. My parents applied for both. As they filled out the work permit application before leaving India, my father explained that she would feel jet lag in the weeks after they arrived in Toronto. The city was ten hours behind Delhi; a different time zone, a different season. Amah just started laughing, her round belly heaved.

"Sahib, everyone knows it's the same time everywhere."

My parents' first home was in a neighbourhood of red brick Victorian houses, professors, artists and ex-hippies. It had two bedrooms, theirs and mine. Amah slept on the floor of the dining room, on a dark brown shag carpet between the radiator and the heavy wooden legs of the mahogany dining table. My first memory of her was as she slept, taking afternoon naps with the sunlight falling across her head, which lay cushioned on an outstretched arm. She kept her long black hair tied in a bun, and her belly gently rose and fell beneath a cotton sari. After she woke up, Amah would let me sit next to her under the dining table and look at the symmetrical tattoos on the top of her hands and feet. Geometric designs in deep indigo, fading into her dark skin. One of our earliest conversations was about how she got them. Amah spoke broken English, Hindi and the south Indian languages of Tamil, Telugu and Kannada. She pointed at her hands and stabbed at the skin with her finger. The tattoos had been done with a sewing needle when she was very young. When she didn't sleep on the dining room floor she slept on a mattress that slid out from beneath my white Ikea bed.

In her twenty-three years in Canada Amah had only two friends. Her first was Lucy, the Italian cleaning lady who came to our house once a week. Lucy was married, but she wore fitted black skirts and sleeveless black blouses as if she were a widow. They would sit on the stairs and talk during Lucy's lunch break, heavy Italian and Indian voices gossiping and complaining about the church. Both women were Catholic. Amah's patron saint was St. Anthony of Padua, a Franciscan always pictured with a child—the infant Jesus—and white lilies in his arms. Amah would sometimes walk the two blocks to Bathurst Street to visit Lucy in a little walk-up across from Steven's Grocery Store. She wore leather chappals on those walks, even in early winter after the first snowfall.

After my parents had made some money we moved up the hill to a neighbourhood with detached houses and wide lawns. Lucy's services were replaced with Louisa's, but in the larger home this relationship was less a friendship than an opportunity for Amah to share the workload and order someone around. It would be where we lived until I went to university, and the last home Amah would know in North America. She graduated from her space on the dining room floor to a stucco apartment in the basement. It suited her—private and dark, with enough space for her two favourite possessions, a television and an altar. She spent her time saying the rosary by candlelight and watching *Magnum P.I.,* her favourite show.

The bedroom opened into a small, windowless antechamber that housed a cedar closet for her cotton saris and luggage. I hung three Indian prints on the wall in an effort to make it more home-like. As a teenager I thought she lived in near poverty; she thought she lived a life of privilege and thanked God every day. Her food, shelter and medical expenses were taken care of and she made weekly phone calls to her daughter Rita in Delhi to make sure the remittances had been received. I had no idea where her other four daughters lived or what they did. Their names were Violet, Mary, Iris and Rose. We heard that Amah's husband died at a home for male beggars in New Delhi a few years after she immigrated, and that Violet died of cancer soon afterwards. The only photo Amah had in her room was a preschool photo of me wearing blue Oshkosh overalls. She kept it in a plastic frame, nailed into the stucco between the television and the altar.

Eleven years after Amah's immigration my parents divorced. Mom moved into a townhouse down the street and for the next seven years Amah, Dad and I would form an unorthodox nuclear family—a south Indian Catholic, a Jew and a lonely child. My bedroom was two floors above Amah's, at the front of the house. In summer the ivy would grow thick and I could barely see outside my bay window. Amah's room became my escape, a safe haven that smelled of must and the betel nut mixed with tobacco that she would chew for a mild high, staining her mouth a permanent red. She became my family then. "Ro mat, beti," she would say, the only woman there to urge me not to cry as she folded her betel nut and tobacco into a paan in the darkness of that basement room.

We spent time together in the kitchen, she on a worn wicker chair pushed against the wall below our wall-mounted phone, me eating her home-made rajma chawal at the white kitchen counter. During Christmas dinner and Passover she refused to eat with us at the same dining table she used to sleep under, instead taking her plate of food to the privacy of her basement room.

Amah decided to retire when I was too old to be fed every meal and when I preferred the company of friends to our shared space in the kitchen. I never thought that she would leave us. It was devastating, but I had little time to consider the vacuum created by her departure to Delhi. Our family friends and neighbours asked after her: "How's Amah?" But my father had already begun searching for a replacement and I just felt hollow whenever her name was mentioned. She had lived in Toronto for thirteen years, a landed immigrant who never chose to sponsor her children.

Amah was replaced by a Jamaican named Angela. She left her six-year-old son behind in Port Antonio to inherit Amah's basement apartment with attached cedar closet. She made the best spaghetti and meat sauce, but she didn't love me. Amah had raised me, rubbing my infant arms with Johnson &

Johnson baby oil to stimulate growth, putting gold jewellery aside for the dowry she imagined I would have as an adult.

Amah-less, I began to notice women always on the move outside my bay window—pushing children in light-framed strollers, helping them out of minivans along with bags of groceries, answering the door in striped-cotton t-shirts and flip-flops. They drove and had friends and went out on weekends (to sing karaoke at the strip malls at Bathurst and Wilson). They were a new kind of Amah, supported by social networks, mobile. Young. Ninety percent of domestic caregivers in Canada were Filipino women, brought into the country by nanny agencies and church networks, Olivias and Joannas who, in the words of one British journalist, "rubbed in the sore point that the feminism of the 1970s would have been broken by the insoluble problem of how to continue career and family if domestic servitude hadn't been neatly passed from one group of women to another."

A young Filipino man was interviewed in the *Georgia Straight* about the difficulties reconnecting with his mother after she sponsored him to Canada. She was required to work twenty-four months in a three-year period before applying for landed immigrant status, and only then was she able to sponsor him. He was six when she left him, twelve when they reunited. The difficulties of their lost time haunted him even in adulthood.

A BBC photographer did a photo essay on a Filipino nanny named Josie Pingkihar, working in Hong Kong. Of the US$470 she made a month, $390 was remitted to her family. With $80 a month in pocket money she cared for a six-year-old Chinese girl and slept on the floor of her bedroom, much like Amah and me. Her own children had started calling her "Aunty." In 2005 Filipino nannies sent home US$10 billion from around the globe. According to the Central Bank of the Philippines, women caring for other women's children contributed 13.2 percent to the country's economic growth. What Josie told the photographer was incredibly insightful: "The government there is not helping us—they have this huge labour export program but they don't create decent jobs at home…Until the government institutes genuine reforms, the Philippines will never recover." Amah had never questioned the opportunities India did or did not give her.

Amah came out of retirement when I was fifteen. She phoned my father from Delhi and told him that she missed me. She moved back as if she'd never left. However, the Amah who came back to a half-empty stucco house was no longer the woman who rubbed my arms with baby oil, but someone I would begin introducing as my grandmother, out of a combination of guilt for having a nanny and pride for someone I loved. She had lived for two years with her daughter Rita and Rita's husband, Cheena.

It was unclear if the money she had earned in Toronto was in her own bank account or theirs.

Amah had aged, and as a result she no longer had specific duties. She would come to my bedroom in the mornings of my years in high school, letting in the dog as she told me to wake up, balancing on the thick soles of her bare feet, which were made rough by years of not wearing shoes. Her place in my room was a pine rocking chair with a quilted floral pillow. She would sit down in the chair and undo the massive bun carefully pinned to the back of her head. Her hair was still black, but thinning. Amah would pull it down past her shoulders and place strands of hair across her lap. She had bulked it up with extensions, bought at a Jamaican hair salon on St. Clair Avenue, down the street from the 7-Eleven. Since none of us knew her age it was estimated to be somewhere around sixty. A birth date was chosen randomly—December 1—halfway between my father's and mine.

As soon as I got my driver's licence, I began driving her to Gerrard Street on the weekends. Saturdays had been her market days, when we would go to Little India for vegetables and bhel poori at Bombay Bhel. Now she would sit peacefully beside me in a sari and green jacket as I drove the two of us down the Danforth. We drank south Indian coffee and ate dosas at the Madras Dhaba. Afterwards we would cruise the video stores for the newest Bollywood titles. It was my way of reconnecting her with her south Indian roots, the next level after hanging Indian prints on her bedroom wall.

After graduating from high school I was accepted into a university in England. The year I left was the year that my father's girlfriend moved in. Amah's work now involved making the occasional cup of tea and cooking whenever she felt the desire to. Her monthly wage remained the same. She continued her walks to the 7-Eleven and Loblaws but she stayed in her basement room more and more. My father and his girlfriend were both empty nesters who had inherited my nanny, and Amah's Tupperwared Indian food remained untouched in the fridge. It was in that year Amah made her second, and last friend, in twenty-three years.

Joanne was completing her doctorate in economics at the University of Toronto. She worked part time as a teaching assistant and part time in my father's office. During my school terms in England, it was Joanne who earned Amah's trust and offered the support I wished I could give her. In the middle of winter, thin, blond Joanne would help Amah, increasingly arthritic, into her second-hand Saab, which smelled of cigarettes, and drive her to Loblaws, or the bank, or Little India.

One holiday, Amah began rubbing her knees and told my father that the flights of stairs had become too much. Whenever I was at home I sat at the foot of her wicker chair and rested my head on her legs, offering to massage them. After all, it was my growing up that led to her redundancy. When I went back to England it was Joanne's idea that she join the South Asian Women's Association. Joanne drove her to a community centre near Bloor and Lansdowne once a month. After the tenth time Amah told Joanne and my father that she didn't want to go back. Why waste her time with a bunch of old women gossiping about their husbands, she said. Hers was already dead. Anyway, he was someone she would rather forget. Amah returned to her basement room, the monthly remittances to Rita and her daily contact with love—Joanne.

Dad told me he was letting go of Amah in the fall. The ivy covering the house had turned and the neighbourhood's nannies were busy seeing their wards off to school. Amah didn't want to go back to India. At twenty-three, I didn't want her to go either. I resented my father for forcing her retirement after two decades of service. She was my grandmother, our responsibility— Amah to countless neighbours and friends. How could she be sent away? But there was no choice. Even though she had savings, she couldn't manage an apartment on her own. Amah had no other friends and family in Canada. No network beyond our house, the 7-Eleven and the discount shops on St. Clair and Gerrard where she would haggle for goods. But there was another reason she had to leave, more painful than the logistics of surviving on her own. I too wanted my own life, and there was no room for my nanny in a grown-up world. I related to Rushdie's narrator in *The Courter*: "For years now I've been meaning to write down the story of Certainly-Mary, our ayah, the woman who did as much as my mother to raise my sisters and me." Twenty-three years after immigrating, Amah would go home to India. Remitted. Returned.

• • •

Laxmi Nagar lies in the north end of New Delhi, on the eastern side of the Jamuna. The lower middle class neighbourhood is squeezed between a congested roadway, funnelling traffic from the bridge, and the exposed sandy banks of the river. It takes forty minutes to reach Amah from my maternal grandparents' home—Amah, my other grandmother, now living in an apartment with her blood daughter. The market below her apartment was crowded with clothing shops and general stores selling her beloved betel nut and tobacco.

The taxi stops in front of a lowrise block of apartments. Rita is waiting at the bottom of a concrete staircase. She is now in her late thirties; a little younger than Amah was when she came to Canada in 1980. She has dark skin and sad eyes. Whenever I phoned for Amah, I spoke to Rita, and now, greeting her, I feel the shame of a cowering dog that knows it has transgressed. Somewhere, I always knew I took this woman's mother away from her. Now, at our convenience, it is this daughter who will care for the aging mother who never wanted to return.

Rita leads me up the stairs to a double entrance, a locked iron gate with a wooden door behind. A young woman answers the door wearing a salwar kameez and dupatta tied as if she's been working, sleeves and hair pulled back. She is Amah's maid, Sangeeta. Amah's own domestic servant. Sangeeta lets us in. The apartment has three bedrooms and a narrow living room painted cream. A small balcony overlooks the telephone lines and market below. One bedroom is Rita's, one is Amah's and the third is devoted to Rita's shrine—an extensive collection of Hindu, Christian and Buddhist images placed in an aluminum mandir.

"Devyani ayaa?" I can hear Amah ask if I've come as Rita leads the way.

"Hah, Amahji." I've come, I say. The only reason my Hindi is alive is because we've spoken together since I was a baby.

She's excited, sitting on her single bed, much thinner than I remember. It has been two years and although I've spoken to her on the phone, I've never met her outside of the home we shared together. Our home.

"Bheto, rani. Bheto." She pats the bed as she barks orders. "Arre Sangeeta, chai banayo!" Someone else can make the tea.

There is a white dog tied outside on the balcony, barking incessantly. Rita's Pomeranian, Lily. There's an Alsatian as well, a large female named Nancy. She sits loyally at Amah's feet and reminds me of the golden retriever Amah left behind. Rita disappears into the kitchen. Only then do I feel comfortable hugging Amah, but what I really want to do is put my head on her lap and sleep like a baby. Instead I examine her room: a television, her own bathroom, a ceiling fan. Screwed into the wall is a white shelf, and on it is her altar, a perfect reproduction of the one in her stucco Toronto room. At least St. Anthony and the Virgin protect her in Laxmi Nagar, I think. There is only one photo on the wall, above a light switch glowing red, and it's of me. It's the same preschool photo in blue Oshkosh that has always been in her room. I wish I could give this woman everything, but I cannot blame my father for wanting his freedom.

"Daddy thik hai? Patricia thik hai?" She listens intently to news from home. "Are you okay, Amah?"

"Kya Karo?" What can I do?, she says. She gives her shoulders a disheartened shrug as she takes betel nut out of a plastic case normally used for film. "Daddy nahin rakha." Daddy didn't keep me.

I listen as she tells me how much she detests India. The food is expensive: rice, meat. The phone gets cut if she doesn't pay extra. She misses Canada. But I look around and she owns this apartment, she has people to care for her, we send her money to help her out, and I realize it's more than food and comfort she craves, it's being Amah. Her home hasn't been taken away from her; her purpose has.

Rita comes in with tea and snacks, and I let go of Amah's hand. Amah gives me a gold necklace with a pendant shaped like three Victoria head coins. She asks me when I'm going to get married.

"When you have a home and husband, I'll come and stay with you," she says, smiling. She chews her paan and refuses to eat, insisting I do. Rita sips her tea and tells me that Amah loves to watch the Discovery channel. When Amah's busy packing away her betel nut and tobacco, Rita looks right at me for the first time, and asks me the only thing she will ever ask me.

"Sponsor me."

Potatoes Cause Brain Tumours
(and Other Things His Mother Told Him)
Natasha Gill

143

The father, his wife and two children are standing in the basement when the bird flies in. It must have come in through the chimney. It circles and circles over their heads, desperately trying to find something familiar and get away from the faux wood panelling and green shag carpet. The bird's circles get closer and closer to the ceiling, its black feathers glistening as if wet. The wife screams, covers her head and runs to the safety of upstairs. The two small daughters stand quietly, their fly-catching mouths open. They are too afraid to move. Don't worry, their huge liquid brown eyes seem to say. Daddy will fix it. They are still at the age when children think their parents are part magic and believe everything they say.

The father's eyes are fixated on the black bird. His thoughts are thousands of miles away. He's thinking of something his mother told him long ago growing up in Murid Wallah, a tiny village in Pakistan. He thinks of the village and the mother he hasn't seen for twenty years. Her words echo in his head: when a bird comes into your house it's a sign of bad luck, a winged messenger sent to share bad news.

• • •

The sun, merciless in the endless green fields, beats down on men darkened by decades of punishing work in the heat. Shirtless, with dirty cotton cloths wrapped around their heads and waists, they hold tightly to plows and trudge slowly in straight lines behind water buffaloes. With each step they stir the earth and release rows of brown, pockmarked spheres. The women, in colourful cotton, are sprinkled like petals over the upturned earth. They bend alongside the freshly turned rows and reach into the earth, pull out handfuls of potatoes and place them into the half-full cotton slings strapped to their backs.

This scene in the field is very familiar. It has been repeated for almost one hundred years. Each year at this time, the villagers work from sunrise to sundown, filling cartload after cartload with potatoes. The men plow the rows and the women and children gather the potatoes and empty them into carts. Once filled, the carts are pulled by donkeys an hour up the dirt road. There the potatoes are filled into trucks and driven away. The men and women of the village have no idea where the potatoes go. For them the journey begins in the earth and ends in the cart.

Most of the children from the village accompany their mothers to the fields. Those too young to walk are left behind to be watched over by the infirm. Children work alongside their mothers, grabbing the smaller potatoes their mothers' eyes have missed and separating the green stalks from the dirt.

A mother and son are working side by side at the far end of one of the rows. She's no more than thirty but all the hard work and the harsh sun make her look much older. She wipes some sweat from her face with the edge of her salwar kameez and turns to look at her son. The boy, as thin as the stalks that surround him, should be in school, but she needs his help. The boy hates to work in the fields and sometimes takes advantage of his mother's kindness to run through the fields playing endless games of hide and seek with some of the other children.

The boy, meanwhile, watches her pull the few last potatoes that he has never tasted: the villagers have developed a fear of potatoes and refuse to eat them. His mother told him missionaries warned the villagers that eating potatoes would cause brain tumours. Instead, he imagines the truckloads are being driven to a big city and being given to well-fed cows owned by rich city people. The cows in his village have to be satisfied with the leftover leaves, stalks and roots the trucks leave behind.

His mother, her cotton sling now full, walks wearily to the cart and empties her last load of the day. "The sun is setting. We have to head home now before it's too dark to see our way." He's happy to hear his mother say these words. Words he has been waiting to hear since they started their work in the blistering heat of the early morning. He had wanted to stay home and read his schoolbooks. He's spent almost the entire day working in the field and, since there is no electricity in the village, he'll have to rely on the fading light from the sun to study.

They begin the long journey home, joining a line of women and children snaking down the dirt path their bare feet have carved along the length of the road. The children laugh and run ahead, relieved that they are now free. The women, too tired to speak, share the quiet pride of a day's work well done.

When they finally reach the village, the mother hurries to boil water and prepare the evening meal for her family. The boy grabs his tattered schoolbook and heads to the open clearing beside the family's tiny house to take advantage of the few minutes of light.

The sights, the sounds and the smells are all so very familiar to him. At night he breathes in dust. In the morning his sheets are dust-covered. He always has a speck of it in his eyes, a powder dusting in his hair and almost always a few grains in his food. He sometimes feels as if he is made of the very same mud that covers the dirt road, the dirt floors and the dirt walls. The dust and he, they are one and the same.

When he isn't helping in the fields, he spends most days in school and every Sunday in the single tiny ramshackle village church built by British and Canadian missionaries. They had been visiting the area and ministering to the population of converted Sikhs since the early 1900s. His grandfather, following the teachings of the missionaries, converted the entire family twenty years before the Partition Massacres. The family, ignored due to their faith, was safe from the Muslim rioters and survived the violence that engulfed most of the region around their village. Unlike many of their Sikh and Hindu neighbours, as Christians they were not forced to relocate with their meager possessions across the new border to India. The missionary visits became sparser after Partition, but the church in the middle of the village always stood as reminder of their presence.

Once, when the boy was only ten, a missionary from Canada visited the village. He had the whitest skin and teeth the boy had ever seen. His clothes were spotless and seemed immune to the dust in the village. He brought a bible for each family and had them gather every evening in the ramshackle church for his sermons. The missionary preached the virtues of being a good Christian from a padded chair by the altar while they sat cross-legged in rapt attention on the dirt floor. He talked about how he felt it was his mission to spread God's word to them. To teach them how to be good Christians. The missionary said good Christians didn't drink or lie, and also, it seemed to the boy, never ate potatoes. The missionary only stayed two months, but his visit survived much longer inside the mind of the boy, who began to dream.

Night became his escape and sleeping on his cot, surrounded by his brothers and sister, he began to dream of Canada. A place free of dust. Filled with clean white faces and clean white clothes. A place where every little boy had a bike, new shoes and a room in a big house filled with books and toys. In his dreams children didn't have to work in fields, and instead spent countless hours reading endless piles of books under bright shining electric lights.

His mother began to encourage his dreams and sometimes she let him leave the fields early so he would have more daylight to study by. "Study hard," she'd say. "Then you can leave this village." She had no idea that her words would send her youngest son away to a place she would never see, a place she probably couldn't even imagine. Soon, he became the top student in his class and was given a chance to go to high school in a larger village near his home. Only one student a year was chosen from his village. He completed high school and learned English, but, of course, there was no money to send him further. His mother was undaunted and a letter was dictated and mailed to a distant uncle in Canada.

"My son would like to come to Canada. He is a top student and has mastered the English language. We do not have the funds for him to continue his education and would like to send him to Canada...Remember, it was I who nursed your sick mother when she was dying. A son should return to bury his mother..."

The guilt, woven into the letter, attached itself to his uncle. A few months later, a letter covered in foreign stamps arrived. His uncle had sent money for a plane ticket to Toronto.

• • •

He's standing in the tiny Faisalabad airport, a three-hour bus journey from his village. The family could not afford to take the entire day off from the fields so only his mother is there to see him off. The others said their good-byes outside the door of the family home. Some cried for him and for the memory of their own unrealized dreams. Others stared at him in awe, wishing they too were on a journey. Mothers pulled their little sons forward, forcing them to say goodbye and urging them to dream.

The flight is boarding. He glances at his mother, hopes her tears have dried. He can barely stand to see her cry but he is glad for these last minutes with her. She asks if he remembers what she has taught him. The places and foods to avoid and the activities he should keep away from. Sermons from his mother and the church resound in his mind. Good people don't drink. They don't dance. They don't smoke. Above all else, he thinks, they never eat potatoes.

As he steps through the glass door and into the passengers-only area of the airport, his mother hands him a tiny bundle. "Take this with you so you will never forget." Embarrassed, he quickly tucks it away, sure it is some of her special spices from home. She is so worried about his meals in Canada. He embraces her and, although he feels the urge, he does not bend down to kiss her tears. The metal doors shut behind him, and he is alone for the first time in his life.

He is excited and apprehensive as he grips his ticket tightly. The importance of the moment escapes him. He has no idea that the plane will be taking him from the land of his birth forever. He will be landing in a place called Toronto. It's a day of many firsts: his first time on a plane and his first time away from his mother, the dust, the fields and the potatoes.

• • •

He has now been working in the restaurant for twenty years but still remembers his first week in his new country. He got off the plane, was questioned by officials for over an hour and then he stood, amidst a churning sea of people outside the airport. No time to talk. No time to help him find his way. One friendly face, a taxi driver from his homeland, spotted his lost look in the crowded arrivals area and immediately recognized the "universal suitcase" of the South Asian immigrant. Old, battered, secured tightly with string and, as a final measure, the owner's destination in large capital letters written in black marker, directly on the suitcase. The driver was kind and, remembering how no one would help him when he arrived, gave him a complimentary ride to downtown Toronto, his uncle's restaurant and his future.

He sat in the front seat of the cab and stared out the window for his first glimpse of his new home. The first surprise was the bitter cold that hit him the moment he stepped outside. He would never forget that cold. There were more surprises through the window of the cab. It seemed to him that there wasn't a speck of colour in this new place. It was a shock after the multi-coloured jewel of his homeland. Everything seemed to be varying shades of grey: the sky, the roads, the buildings, even the people. There was also a solid grey needle surrounded by other tall grey buildings, dominating the approaching skyline. Where was the green, he wondered. Where was the sun? The warmth was even missing from his uncle, who expected him to work endless shifts at the restaurant to pay back the airfare. Out of pride he washed dish after dish, cup after cup, endless piles of spoons and forks without complaint, never sure how many piles would equal his freedom.

His first few days working in the restaurant held the biggest surprise. He discovered that Canadians ate potatoes! Either they didn't know about the brain tumours, or they did and they were immune. They ate them fried, baked, mashed, grilled, boiled. They seemed to eat them with everything, for lunch and for dinner. There were piles and piles of them in the restaurant, the grocery stores and corner markets. He washed them, peeled them and cut them. He still couldn't bring himself to eat them. Surprisingly, everyone, even his rich uncle, laughed in his face when he tried to warn them about the dangers of the potatoes. Perhaps his uncle had been away from home for too long and forgotten everything his own mother told him.

The realization came slowly: maybe his mother wasn't right. Maybe potatoes didn't cause brain tumours. Maybe the missionaries wanted to keep the potatoes all to themselves. Maybe eating potatoes made you rich and white. It broke his heart to think of how she would feel if she knew what he now knew. His dreams changed and at night he now dreamt of his mother, his family, his village and the dust.

◆ ◆ ◆

The news the bird wanted to share comes the next day. The phone rings early the next morning. The father says hello, then shouts hello a few times more. He starts to speak rapidly in a language his wife and children do not understand and then hangs up. Something his mother warned him about actually came true. The bird did bring bad news on its dark wings. His mother has died.

At that moment, he remembers the tiny bundle she gave him when he left Pakistan all those years ago. It has rested untouched in the suitcase he carried with him. He hasn't been on a journey since he came to Canada, so the battered suitcase sits, waiting in the closet. He carefully opened the bundle. It was full of dust, dust from the village.

Now he knows no matter how hard he tries he will never escape the dust. It has made him and it is something he will never wash away.

Blood Rivers
Gein Wong

There was no need to open my eyes to tell the difference; all I needed to do was breathe. One slow inhalation of air held in my body as long as possible. At the time, I couldn't articulate exactly what it was, but what I could say was that with one deep breath my lungs were filled with the atmospheric odours particular to Hong Kong. The emphasis is on the word "particular." It's not pungent or sweet, not rancid or polluted, just particular and entirely different from the air I was used to breathing in Toronto. These are things I can tell you about Hong Kong air. It is certainly much more humid and dense. And the particles of pollution that mingle amongst the oxygen, carbon dioxide and ozone are more intense and intimidating. But as the air filtered through each vacuole of my lungs I began to get this subtle sense that Hong Kong air is also filled with something that isn't so scientific, that doesn't just arouse the odour receptors in my nose, but rather touches on something more intrinsic to my being. As our plane landed at Hong Kong International airport that spring day, I knew the exact moment that the plane doors opened and Hong Kong air entered the cabin. I wanted to hold my breath for as long as possible, absorb as much as possible from that virgin breath of air.

"AHHHHHHHH!"—a collective scream of joy my father and my aunt made as they saw each other in the arrivals area of the airport. It was the type of scene you would expect when a brother and sister see each other for the first time in 30 years. My aunt hugged my father for what seemed like an eternity. My mother stood by and made sure our luggage was still in place. My aunt then hugged me, and handed me a welcoming present—a pen. This wasn't an ordinary writing utensil; it was meant to be a symbolic gift, though at the time I had no idea what message my aunt was intending to convey. On first glance the pen was nothing special, a thin and cheap plastic model; you twisted the body until the ballpoint extended out of the tip. On the pen was a drawing of celebratory red and yellow fireworks, as well as the words "Hong Kong 1997."

1997. This was not a good number for my family or for many people in Hong Kong. For some it would be a number of reunification and a home-coming; for others a number of anxiety, fear and the desire to run. It was the year the British Empire would relinquish control of Hong Kong and return it to China, the contemplation of which had left families wondering what would happen to the Hong Kong they knew and loved under Chinese rule.

That year had been an impetus for migration, a hi-tech time bomb that grabbed hold of the fear residing in the minds of my family and transplanted many of them to North America. 1997 is a major reason why I type these words in English, why I drink purified water from Lake Ontario, why my passport says Canada on it and why Hong Kong air seemed so distanced and foreign.

My father didn't share any stories of Hong Kong with me. I knew vague tidbits about Hong Kong, how my relatives used to be farmers, how my father loved to swim, how he used to sit at the side of a dirt road to eat dusty noodles for lunch. For 30 years, my relatives had asked for my father to return to Hong Kong and it wasn't until 1997, just before the handover and just after my grandmother had spent three weeks in the hospital, that he finally decided to take us to the land where he grew up.

My grandmother was a car ride away in Kowloon. When we got to my aunt's car, my mother and I squeezed ourselves into the backseat. Even though I was only a child my knees almost touched the back of the passenger's seat. My father accidentally got into the driver's seat. My aunt chuckled and told him this wasn't Canada and that they drove on the opposite side of the road in Hong Kong, just like the British. She took out her wallet and tipped the boy who helped us carry out our bags, handing him the money as if it was nothing more than scrap paper. When my aunt started up the car, there was a Chinese song on the radio, but she quickly put in a CD of the Beatles. "I remember your father used to love listening to this album," she said.

My aunt talked non-stop throughout the entire ride. Her accent was nothing like what my parents sounded like when they spoke Cantonese. Her words were sharper, quicker and much more confident. She constantly smiled and laughed and recounted stories that were filled with what seemed like an endless amount of happiness and success. My cousin went to the same school that my father went to and she was the top student in her class. They had just had a celebratory dinner the week before, because she had won a prestigious English-language award. My aunt made a point to slow down the car when we passed my father's old school: a plain, box-shaped building at the corner of the street with brick walls painted white. If you looked closely, you could see the paint lay uncomfortably on the surface of the brick.

During that car ride I only opened my mouth twice to ask my father questions. The first thing I asked him was the location of the river where he used to swim every day after school. He looked at me, puzzled. He paused, looked off in the distance as if to relocate this body of water, and then said that he would point it out when we were close to it. Ten minutes later, he pointed westward out the window, but I didn't see a river; all I saw was concrete and high-rise buildings. At the time, I wondered whether he had misheard me or maybe I had mispronounced the word "stream" in Cantonese. I could have easily mixed up the word for stream with the word for staircase.

"Your father used to be more like a fish than anything else, he always swam in that river," my aunt said.

At this point, I hesitated several times before asking my father the second question: "Baba, where is the family farm?" I thought this was a simple question that my father would answer with a quick response, but the following moments of silence stretched longer then I expected. Even my aunt did not have anything to say in response. My father pressed his hand against his chin, made a sharp grunting sound and then began rubbing the palm of his hand along his jaw line. As he turned to look out the window, a hint of anger crossed his face. "We already passed the family farm," he said, but this made no sense to me. During our entire trip, we had not passed anything resembling farmland, or so I had thought. All we had driven by were urban buildings, modern highways and concrete sidewalks. But I didn't ask him to explain because sharing stories was not a skill my parents used very often.

Even though my grandmother had lived with us in Canada for the first few years of my life, I didn't really remember very much. I had one definite memory of her and several vague fragments that were as much use as random pieces of a jigsaw puzzle. But in 1997, my impressions of her grew exponentially. By this time she was so frail that she struggled to walk with the help of a cane. She spent most of her time in her compact rectangular apartment, sitting in her shallow bamboo rocking chair with a floral printed cushion along the seat and backrest. A lunar calendar hung on an aged and rough wooden wall, a potted plant sat on the narrow window sill and a small battery-powered radio constantly emitted the sounds of Chinese opera. But she had parted with most of her personal belongings. My cousin later told me that she was often very tired and rarely laughed. The hope she had for a bright successful future for my father and his family had faded away and been replaced with the bite of a reality that had left her worn down and lonely. However, I met an entirely different woman when we arrived in Hong Kong. On that day she was filled with elation. She reached out for my father's hand and patted it, grasping onto his forearm as if it was a lifeline flung into the Hong Kong harbour. My father made a motion as if he were going to hug my grandmother, but I could see his hesitation, afraid he would hurt her frail body. He said something tenderly to my grandmother and then pointed in my direction. My grandmother looked at me with a degree of happiness I had never thought possible before. When our eyes met I peered into the deepest and most familiar soul I had ever encountered.

• • •

"Come with me to the rooftop," my grandmother said. She grabbed her cane and gently rose from her rocking chair. She headed over to the jagged and dusty stairwell in the corner of the room and began climbing the stairs. I watched her as she gingerly took each step, my aunt standing two steps behind her ready to catch her in case she fell. *"Ah Ma*...careful... slowly now...," my aunt kept repeating in a sharp cautious tone. Everyone in the room let out a brief cry of concern as my grandmother stumbled for a moment. My aunt reached forward, grabbed her by the waist and said, *"Ah Ma*, you don't need to go up, we can sit in the living room." My grandmother turned around with a look of determination in her eyes. "We are all going to the roof," she commanded.

When she reached the top of the stairs, we all followed her onto the rooftop. There was a stool at the far end. On it stood a bowl of rice patted down into the shape of a cone. There was also a plate of chicken, some incense and a few objects I didn't recognize. I didn't understand and I looked at my father to see if he knew what was happening. As my father looked down at me, the edges of his lips raised slightly into a small and tight smile. He leaned over, put his hand on top of my head and whispered to me, "It's an old Buddhist ritual."

"What kind of ritual?" I asked.

He paused for a moment. "Grandma probably wants to welcome us home."

Everyone stood around and waited for my grandmother to walk over to the bowl of rice. I watched her as she made her way to the display, resting her body on her cane in between each step. Off in the distance was the mountainous terrain of Hong Kong; somewhere in those mountains was an ancient Buddhist temple I had read about. From my angle, it looked as if my grandmother was slowly making her way up those mountains. When she got to the stool she turned around and smiled at us. My father and my aunt smiled back, but they didn't move. She took the bowl of rice and began pressing down on it with her fingers. My grandmother turned around again, but this time she didn't look at us, she looked at the ground right behind her. It was at this point that everyone started walking towards her. She began saying something, but I couldn't make out the words. I looked at my aunt for answers, but she just smiled and shrugged her shoulders.

◆ ◆ ◆

My grandmother prayed on that rooftop for a long time, her right hand clenched tightly with her left hand covering it—one large fist that she rocked back and forth. The others copied the motion with their hands but they couldn't copy the passion on my grandmother's face.

I closed my eyes and began rocking my hands. But I didn't just pretend and play along with things. I listened to everything my grandmother was saying. Her thick *dong guan* accent gave each word a heavy lilt and a syrupy feel. Even though I was so young, I knew this moment would never be repeated. I let every syllable pour into my being, settling firmly and permanently in my mind.

There's one other memory of my grandmother that I hold onto tightly, even today years after that visit in 1997. The memory comes to me every time I walk into my apartment and look at the rocking chair in my living room. The wooden frame has aged and the varnish is wearing away from years of use and travel. I have moved that rocking chair with me from rundown house to mouse-infested dwelling, to college dorm, to basement apartment to ground-floor apartment, to high-rise apartment. Loaded it into the back of one station wagon and two rental vans, carried it up five flights of stairs, moved it ten blocks down a major street and squeezed it into three elevators. The fabric covering the cushions is a tell-tale sign that this chair is from the 1970s, the cushions being the cloth version of wood panelling. Its look clashes with the artsy and modern decor of the rest of my living area, and I can see people questioning my sense of taste and design in their silent look.

But when I look at that chair I don't think about dated fashion. I think about changing times: I think of history, and of my grandmother. She's sitting in that chair, using her feet to propel the rocking motion of the chair, but I don't see her feet, because my eyes are closed and I'm enjoying the undulating motion she creates. I'm lying against her torso and I'm clinging to her like a blanket pulled tight against a motel bed. I can feel her breath touch the top of my head. Some of the air slides down the back of my neck, while the rest is absorbed into the pores of my skin and spreads through the blood rivers of my body. She is speaking softly to herself because she thinks I am sleeping and she doesn't want to wake me. But no matter how much she tries, I can hear her. I can hear the Buddhist prayer she is reciting, I can hear her words about Hong Kong, about the river my father learned to swim in, about all the things she feared that no one would tell me. She whispers about how the soil and land that made up the farm was no longer a part of our family. How my grandfather's brother had already sold the land off to developers who wanted to build high-rise housing and malls. About how, in doing so, my grandfather's brother kept all the money to himself, leaving my grandfather with nothing. About how close they used to be, but how money brings out a different side of some people, especially when someone has virtually nothing and money suddenly falls from the skies.

As this memory begins to sputter out I hear these last sentences from her: "Even though we will not know each other, I am going to miss you," she says. "Listen to your father, listen to your mother, listen because..."

That's all I remember.

◆ ◆ ◆

I think this is a memory from my childhood. But it's a memory I'm not sure that I have. That I'm not sure is real. I believe it's a memory of my grand-mother, but part of me thinks I am wrong. Part of me doubts I ever felt her breath touch me. I question my own version of reality because growing up I had no other memory of my grandmother. She lived in our house when I was a baby and left before I could say my first word in Cantonese. In my mind, she is there for that one brief moment in my life. One minute her wisdom is swirling about me, the next minute she is gone. At my parents' home, there is no bed for her, nor are there any pictures of us together in the family photo album. She was not there when I started kindergarten, or when I first picked up a plastic shovel to help my father shovel snow off the driveway. I don't know how I know all these things about my family's life in Hong Kong, but somehow I do, and it must be because my grandmother told me. This memory is something I want so badly, I don't know if I sacrificed reality in order to create it. This memory is something I need to have, something I rely on.

Caribana
Denise Barnard

159

In the summer of 1977, almost a year after Elvis's death, I met my father for the first time. While many were still mourning the passing of "the King," in Toronto, we were preparing for a party that promised to be hotter than the record temperatures that divided the city into those who loved the heat and those who didn't. Almost everything I knew about Albert Godfrey was twenty years out of date. His lean, compact build, easy smile, slick razor cut, natty clothes and Ray-Ban shades had been captured in a snapshot taken on a hot day in 1958, not long before I was born. For me, those details were as close as I thought I'd ever come to knowing my father. Until that August morning when I rode the revolving door into the Sheraton Centre Hotel.

There he was, looking around the lobby anxiously. I could hardly breathe. When he saw me, a grin hijacked his face; I hadn't seen anyone that happy in a long time. I swallowed hard, my stomach churning with fear and excitement, my throat dry. As we shook hands, the warmth of his palm against mine, he leaned in close and kissed me on the cheek. And for that brief moment, I found myself believing in God—something I hadn't done since I was a kid.

"I cyant believe we both really here," he said. His voice was soft and breathless like he'd just had the wind knocked out of him, too. Around us, voices rose and fell amid laughter and a baby's cries. It felt as though we'd walked into a surprise party in our honour. My father shuffled from one foot to the other, and when our eyes met, he smiled shyly, uncertainly. I smiled back, and pointed to two seats in a quiet corner.

Albert stroked the leather armrest of his chair and asked me about Toronto, as though it was on the other side of the world instead of just across the border. He was surprised when I explained that the Arctic was the only cold place in Canada during the summer. I couldn't help laughing. He stared at me blankly, then chuckled and began playing with a piece of lint on his pant leg. I studied his rough big-knuckled fingers, trying in vain to pair them with the delicate, flowery signature on the back of his photo. From there, I moved on to his hair, which was a maze of grey and black, and his marble-smooth skin. But it was my father's nose I will always remember. Demanding more than its share of space, his bulbous nose was a touch Cyrano de Bergerac, but with none of the French romantic's famed ugliness. I stroked my own, a smaller version of his. He was more handsome than he deserved to be, I thought, as though looks depended on actions.

"Yuh prettier than in pictures," he said suddenly.

"Pictures? What pictures?" I snapped.

"The ones I," he paused, licked his lips, "ask yuh motha for send me. A new one every yea—"

I clenched my fists to keep my hands from shaking. "Why didn't you just call or write? At least I would have known you were alive."

He hung his head, and mumbled something about not wanting to make things worse. By then, the veins in my skull felt like they were pumping something heavier than blood.

"I always know how yuh doin'. If anythin' happen to yuh, I woulda been there."

But what was the point in explaining that he'd already missed so much—the parent-teacher nights my mother attended alone, the Father's Day cards I made in grade school, my high school graduation speech. The summer I was fourteen, I dug through every drawer, shelf and hiding spot in her bedroom until I found a shoebox older than me in the back of the closet. For months afterward, I kept the stolen photo tucked under my pillow, looking at my father before I went to bed each night. His level gaze directed at the camera, the whiteness of his shirt and the perfect cut of his dark suit, worn with ease, as though he dressed like this every day. He'd seemed so cool and in control then, as though he could do anything.

"Gem, is sorry me sorry for all these years. Me dint mean for let yuh down."

His eyes were so sad, I felt tears gathering behind my own. I bit my lip, stared at the carpet and silently counted backward from ten—a habit I'd developed as a child. When I finished, I said, "We're here now. That's what matters."

He nodded for what seemed a long time, as though he didn't trust himself to speak.

"Why don't we go and see the parade?" I stood up and waited for him to do the same, but instead, he began talking about how his wife, Evelyn, would never have spoken to him again if he hadn't brought her to Toronto, since there was no Caribana in New York.

"But I tol' her for remember is me day wid me daughta. I hope yuh don' mind too much."

I shook my head slowly, and watched him get to his feet.

"Ev and Clary cyant wait for meet yuh. I go get them an' then we go."

Who's Clary, I wondered, as my father disappeared into a crowd of slack-jawed boys in baseball caps and loud teenage girls in Afros and Farrah Fawcett flips.

• • •

Evelyn wore a T-shirt that read NEW YORKERS COME IN TWO KINDS: LOUD AND LOUDER. She was an Amazon, at least six feet tall, which brought my head to her chest as she pulled me into a bear hug. "Now this is a picture," she said, the word sounding more like "pitcher." She clapped her hands. "Ya look lovely."

I said thank you, though I was embarrassed by her praise. I wore a faded coral peasant blouse, yellow flares and old Jesus sandals my mother always threatened to throw out. I hadn't wanted to dress up and risk looking like a fool, but now that seemed like a poor excuse. Even Clarice, who was a kid, seemed to think so, the way she frowned at me.

"Clarice, cat got ya tongue? Where's ya hello for Gem?" Evelyn said.

The little girl said hello, and then turned to my father. "Albee, is it time to go yet?"

At his nod, Clarice's expression softened into a happy leer. Something I associated with parties and adults who'd had too much to drink. She was good at getting what she wanted, and she knew it. My father smiled, reached for her hand, and the two of them walked away. In her red, green and gold outfit, Clarice looked like gaudy Christmas wrap.

"Only nine and she got G wrapped round her little finger," Evelyn said. "I swear sometimes you'd think it was her Mr. Godfrey was married to instead o' me."

With his squared shoulders and gentle swagger, my father had the natural charm of a man who could divide the women in his life as easily as the heat wave did Torontonians. In his powder-blue silk shirt and beige dress pants, Albert could have been headed for an air-conditioned concert at the O'Keefe Centre instead of the sweltering heat of the Caribana parade.

• • •

Outside, people strolled down the middle of Queen Street. It was one of the few days in the year when Toronto forgot its dull Protestant roots. Across from the hotel, colourful booths dotted the usually grey Nathan Phillips Square, and the air smelled of curry and fried fish. The clock at Old City Hall chimed, but it couldn't compete with the lively steel drums we could hear from two blocks away on University Avenue.

"Toronto seems like a nice town," Evelyn said.

I nodded, and agreed that it was, not bothering to add that it was, in fact, a city. In those days, with bars still closing early and people smiling whenever they asked me where I was from, Toronto often felt like a big small town.

When we reached the parade, Evelyn said, "This is one classy street. Reminds me of, ya know, grand ol' Park Av'nue in Manhattan."

I'd never seen Park Avenue, but I'd always thought of University as dignified and sombre, sleepy even—home to Toronto's four big hospitals and the American embassy. People usually seemed insignificant next to the stone memorials for heroes of the first and second World Wars. But today, warriors, mermaids, dragons and sea gods floated down one side of the double boulevard, waving to the roaring crowd. Handsome bronze-painted mas band players and sequinned beauty queens in peacock blue and green stirred up the mood even more with mesmerizing gyrations that would have put a young Elvis to shame.

Evelyn, Albert and Clarice grooved to the beat effortlessly. I wasn't much of a dancer, but it didn't take long to, in my mother's words, "fin' me feet." The rhythm tickled my soles, and from there travelled through my legs, hips, chest and arms until it totally infused my body like some sort of potent spell or herb. For other partiers, that elixir sloshed around in wineskins that dangled from their necks, wrists and belt loops.

Down below on University Avenue, bare-chested men lassoed their women with the mesh tank tops they'd left home wearing, while women flashing skin like it was easy money danced hip to hip or crotch to crotch with man-sized lizards, frogs and bees. A spirit on stilts teetered past, a red-lipped grin contorting his masked face, his teeth a bright half moon against his dark plastic skin.

Next up was a sea lobster with a strap-on dildo so huge I winced. The minute Evelyn saw him, she clamped a hand over her tinted glasses. I laughed, tempted to lean over and see if she really had her eyes closed or whether she was watching every move his dildo made. We'd barely stopped laughing when a mermaid and fisherman appeared.

The mermaid's costumed skin shone slickly, as though she'd just arrived fresh from the sea. Her dyed weave bounced in time with her breasts, and she flicked an ample tail at the husky bowlegged fisherman in his tatty straw hat, top and shorts. Whenever he tried to kiss her, she shrugged away with a roll of her eyes. On his third try, the dainty mermaid gave the fisherman a shove that toppled him to the ground as easily as a cardboard cutout. People gasped, a few even hissed, although he was on his feet in seconds, smirking and hugging the mermaid, like he'd already won her heart. But she took her time, batting her eyelashes with dizzying speed. Then, slowly, she removed her hands from her hips and surrendered, letting the fisherman kiss her long and hard to a serenade of cheers and whistles.

◆ ◆ ◆

In between floats, Albert scanned the crowd as though expecting to see someone he knew. "The parade remind me of Carnival in Antigua," he explained.

I nodded. "The first Caribana was in 1967."

"Almos' ten years. Was a good idea judgin' from all the people."

"Maybe I can persuade Mom to come next year."

"Lil use for love Joovay morning. Bands playin', people dancin' in the streets before the sun even rise," Albert said, staring into the distance. "Was one big party, the place to be when we were young."

Young? It was hard to imagine. "Mom hardly ever talked about you. When she mentioned your name a few days ago, I thought you were dead."

"Dead," Albert flinched. "That's what me get, I guess, for bein' such a jackass all these years."

Lillian must have loved or hated my father terribly—or perhaps both. Whenever I asked about him, she said there wasn't much to tell, except one time when she said Albert was the sort of man that most people liked. "What part of New York do you live in?" I asked.

"Brooklyn. Yuh ever been there?"

I shook my head. The farthest I'd ever been was Niagara Falls, an hour and a half from Toronto by car.

"Yuh have for visit then. If is awright wid yuh motha, that is."

"I'm not a kid anymore. Besides, our apartment doesn't feel that big these days."

"When yuh graduate, will be time for look for yuh own place."

I stared at him. "Graduate? How did you know?"

"Me have friends in high places," he joked, gazing at the sky. "So how yuh enjoyin' school?"

"It's..." I paused, momentarily torn between the complex truth and a simple lie, "more work than I expected, though I'm learning a lot." Glen, my former tutorial leader, now lover, saw to that. But I didn't bother to elaborate. He was a part of my university experience, like smoking pot, which I'd leave behind before long.

After that, our conversation returned to the subject of the weather—and the parade, which my father believed was vital on a day like this. The perfect distraction from the heat, he said. As we looked around, I noticed the swaying bodies and half-closed eyes of people dancing to a rhythm in their heads. I shut my eyes, losing myself in the ether of sound, and when I finally opened them, Clarice and Evelyn had returned from the washroom. We listened to Evelyn complain about the long lineups, while Clarice sulked after Albert refused to carry her on his shoulders.

"Yuh too ole for that. Come stand here," he said, motioning to a spot beside him.

As I moved over, I took in Clarice's sloped chin, large eyes and peach-pit-coloured skin. There wasn't the slightest resemblance between her and my father, though he treated her like his daughter, while he and I were family, and strangers at the same time.

All of a sudden, Clarice yelled "Look!" and pointed at the street.

Gossamer wings, shimmering haloes and dazzling white teeth added to the unearthly beauty of five leggy women in glittering second-skin bodysuits. Next to me and Evelyn, three men in "We Be Jammin'" T-shirts, fanny packs and knee shorts wore dreamy looks as the women, breasts heaved as high as their stiletto heels, blew kisses. Even the most evil bastard would become a saint if one of these beauties was waiting for him in heaven, I bet. Evelyn smiled, as though she'd read my thoughts.

"G never likes the angel on our Christmas tree. But somethin' tells me he'd like one of these better." She winked.

I laughed, glad my father hadn't come alone after all.

The angels started shrieking. Seconds later, the devil strutted out of a mist of dry ice, a microphone in his hand. Red horns sprung from his dreadlocks, a pointed tail from the tight black jumpsuit that showed off his tall broad-shouldered frame.

"How everybody feelin'?" he bellowed, his amplified voice deep and sexy.

"Good!" and "Hot!" people yelled. One bold woman shouted, "Hot for you, hon'!" The devil shook his pitchfork in the air with a satisfied grin, and women in the audience cheered.

"Glad to hear it 'cause I'm here to make sure all the party people feelin' hot, whether you're from Antigua, T&T, Jamaica, Grenada, Martinique, Barbados, Dominica, Ghana!" He paused after each country, while people raised their hands and whooped with pride. "And let's not forget Brixton, the Bronx, and Scarborough, Ontario."

After the applause ended, the music picked up and the chorus line of angels kicked up their legs. Around me, the din of voices swelled with the same comforting quality as Evelyn's hug, and for a moment, I felt an unexpected, overwhelming surge of happiness.

• • •

By five, the crowds on University Avenue had thinned out, but Queen Street hummed with tired partiers. Garbage cans lining the sidewalk overflowed like mini Mount Vesuviuses. We detoured through Osgoode Hall, which looked like both paradise and prison with its pristine gardens and high, spiked black iron fence.

"They make these entrances them small-small," Albert said, manoeuvring his way through the boxy gate after me.

"They were built to keep the cows out."

"Cows?" Clarice giggled.

"It's hard to imagine now, isn't it?"

"That's what yuh call progress." Albert laughed. "Yuh know yuh history awright."

"It's going to be my major," I said, surprising myself. The decision I'd been thinking about for months suddenly made.

"Ya picked yaself a good field," Evelyn said. "This world's full of history."

Sunlight glanced off the solid stone buildings bordered by a cobbled walkway, a band of glossy flowers and shrubs, stately trees and a sparkling lawn. Evelyn slowed, and we all lingered, watching its perfection slowly dim until Clarice announced she was hungry.

By the time we reached the hotel, cars thronged the street in a temporary traffic jam. The happy faces of just a few hours ago were replaced by a more sober crowd, who knew nothing of the spell that had briefly transformed the city and brought it to life. As I listened to Albert and his family talk about going home the next morning, I knew I couldn't go back to the hotel with them. I wanted to say goodbye out here, where the remaining light and heat, and even the garbage, reminded me of the fun we'd had.

"I should get going," I said.

"So soon? We'd love to have ya stay." When Evelyn saw that I wasn't going to change my mind, she said, "Well, don't be a stranger, otherwise we'll come and find ya, won't we, Clary?" Clarice nodded and smiled at me for the first time that day. She and Evelyn waved as they went into the hotel. My mother would have liked them, I thought.

I returned my father's smile before we both glanced away. He looked tired, older than he had just a few hours ago, but more real to me than he'd ever been.

"Prob'ly a good idea not for push our luck," Albert said, though he was clearly disappointed. "We did good for two people no see each other in almos' twenty years, eh?"

I inhaled deeply and nodded as a guy in a T-shirt that said "Elvis lives" walked by. "Yes," I said, hoping luck wouldn't desert us like it had the King. "Yes, we did."

The Call
of the Mountain
Rabindranath Maharaj

169

Every time Billy Bilkim Costanza entered the antique shop where I worked, he would find some excuse to say, "The mountain still calling me, boy. The voice in my ears might change but the message always remains the same. Always the same." Sometimes he would pretend he was examining one of the old, creaky lamps that Mr. Pervez, the owner of the shop, had bought at a garage sale and whisper gloomily, "I don't think it's a good idea to ignore the mountain. I might be playing with fire." Then his gaze would shift from the cluttered shop with its cracked teapots and freckled brass decanters to the door facing Albert Street. He never stayed longer than twenty minutes or so.

Costanza was different from all the other customers, not only because he never made a single purchase, but also in the way he would frequently gaze outside and breathe in little gulps, as if he was suffocating or hiding from someone. And he always left in a big hurry.

One night in May, about four months after Costanza's first appearance in the shop, I saw him digging into a box with ugly paintings of cactus plants and desert flowers. His nostrils were twitching as if he was trying to smell the flowers. I waited until his examination was over before I asked what had been on my mind for so long, "Tell me Mr. Costanza...is somebody looking for you?"

He drew himself to his full medium height and blew into his clasped palms as if he was rehearsing a long speech. Even though the night was cool, small drops of sweat were running down his fleshy neck. "The mountain doesn't forget, boy. It has many, many friends. Even in this overcrowded place." He glanced swiftly through the door. "They could be anywhere. Anywhere."

I tried not to smile at Costanza's habit of repeating some of his words. "And they are looking for *you*? What mountain crime did you commit?"

It was a mistake to speak this lightly because Costanza left so hastily he almost dislodged a row of porcelain angels set upon the wooden frame of an overturned couch. After he had left, I saw Mr. Pervez standing stiffly before his cubicle office at the back of the shop. "So you had some nice little chats with Mr. No-buy-anything-at-all? Yes?" Whenever Mr. Pervez tried to be mocking, his voice would lift to just a few notes below a shriek. "And what, please tell, did you talk about today that was so interesting?"

I knew he would be confused if I mentioned Costanza's mountain, so I told him, "The usual. Old this and that." This was a favourite expression of Mr. Pervez but he did not like to hear anyone else using it.

"Old this and that, eh? Now please carry old this and that cash register to back office. Or are you too tired from so many chats?"

I heaved his old, bulky adding machine, which weighed close to fifty pounds, to his small, dirty back room. I heard him grumbling about "useless no buy customers" before he broke into his strange foreign language. A few minutes later, I saw him trying to drape the "closed" sign around the neck of a Mexican statue in the little glass case facing Albert Street. When I left, he was still grumbling and manhandling the poor statue.

Mr. Pervez was never in a good mood but he was especially short tempered following each of Costanza's visits. And the strange part was that both men with their neat bellies and sad, faraway looks could have passed for brothers. Yet I cannot recall a single word ever passing between the two. Sometimes while I was listening to Costanza, I would see Mr. Pervez standing gruffly before his back office and I would think of two fat, retired boxers squaring each other up. I often wondered if they had adopted that same stance before I began working at the antique shop.

I felt that they could be friends if only they knew more of each other. This thought was running through my mind when, a week later, Mr. Pervez asked what was so interesting about Costanza for me to ignore the other customers. I decided against mentioning that the shop was usually empty because that was a sore point with Mr. Pervez. Instead, I slipped out some-thing about the mountain.

Instantly Mr. Pervez was alert. "Mountains? What damn craziness is that? What so special about this mountains?" Although I didn't know one single thing about the mountain, not its name or even where it stood, I said that the people there never climbed down their entire lives because once they did they could never return. I think I wanted the mountain to seem special but Mr. Pervez was not impressed. "Is this all he told you? This damn nonsense?"

Some of his alarm faded away. "That they only have climb-down muscles in their foot? Maybe is a special kind of polios." He broke into a broad, horrible smile that caused the mole on his cheek to creep closer to the nest of hair in his ear. "Polios for peoples who only walking backwards."

Just before closing time, while I was lugging the cash register to the back, he told me gleefully, "Careful. Careful you don't strain your climb-down muscles."

The next day he wasn't in such a good mood. He stormed into the shop and didn't seem to care when he brushed a Russian doll that clattered to the floor, spilling all its little babies. "The worst peoples on the face of the earth is the polices. For one hour the polices only listen to the white lady who was driving as if she own the roads. One hour. Count it!" He held up his stubby ring-filled fingers before me. "And for Mr. Pervez, less than five minutes." He always talked like this, putting himself as another person when he was distressed. "Tell me, Sammy. Is something wrong with my Englishes? Do Mr. Pervez look like some kind of common crooks?" He unbuttoned his trench coat and fled to his office.

Now I don't want to give the impression that Mr. Pervez was racist or anything because he hated with the same dose anyone who came into the shop without buying anything. He was always polite to their faces though, pretending to be from India or Turkey or Afghanistan or Venezuela and many places in the atlas, but the minute they left empty-handed he would tell me, "I hope you learn a good lesson today, Sammy. Never trust anybody from India. Their main aim in life is to find fault and complain." Sometimes he made a puppet with his hand opening and closing his fingers. "Pok-pok-pok."

I know I shouldn't find this funny because it was sad in a way to see Mr. Pervez so disappointed after he had spent sometimes half an hour talking in his fake Persian or Pakistani accent. And he always balanced out his quarrels by later bad-mouthing people from other places too. Polish, Chinese, Jamaicans, Russians, everyone who was not born in Canada set his teeth on edge. During my first week at the shop, about five months earlier, he had laid down a list of rules, which, he said, had been repeatedly broken by his previous employees. "And guess where lazy workers are now?" he had asked cheerfully. But I soon realized that his quarrels were really a kind of showing-off. Just to prove how important he was.

This bad mood with the police was different, though. It lasted all day. In the night, he stormed out of his office to complain once more about this injustice to his spotless driving record. He didn't say a word to me; instead he argued with a row of sleepy-looking plastic Buddhas about the condition of his life, his ungrateful children, his mounting debts, his ulcers. "I have half a mind to go back home," he grumbled to a Buddha. "Pervez just gives the polices there a bribe and everything fixed. No tickets, no bothers, no bony white ladies." Whenever he ran into some sort of problem, the first words that dropped from his mouth were to go back home, which was strange in a way because he always complained about other people who dressed and spoke as if they were "still minding goats and sheep."

After he had returned to his office, I noticed Costanza quietly inspecting a rusty stethoscope at the other end of the shop. I did not see him enter because I was so distracted by Mr. Pervez's quarrelling. He asked what was bothering Mr. Pervez and I said the police.

"Police? What did they want from him? Were they here in the shop?" Only when I explained that Mr. Pervez had some sort of traffic accident did he relax a bit. Still, that same night, I noticed a new slice of nervousness in the way Costanza took off his gloves and blew on his palms and cracked his fingers. I had never observed his fingers before. They were long and slim and didn't match his body at all. I also noticed the thin lines that split all his nails like hooves. When he noticed me staring, he hurriedly replaced his gloves and asked if I had ever observed anyone acting strange in the shop.

To tell the truth everyone who came into the shop was strange. There was the hunched man who rode on his bike whether it was snowing or not. He came into the shop with his helmet on, which made him look like a sleepy turtle. He worked at the Toronto Reference Library and he bought many of the old books Mr. Pervez had picked up at garage sales for a quarter or less. Then there was the old woman with the frizzy hair and all the beads around her neck. Her lips were always red and her soft little-lady voice would some-times get hoarse and low like those women sports announcers on television. She was interested only in necklaces and bracelets. There was also the fat, blocky man who leaned on his walking stick and gazed for an hour or more at the painting of a half-naked woman holding a bowl of fruits, and the bald-headed Italian who was always sniffing and rubbing his nose while he complained about the ugly new buildings going up across the city. I think Mr. Pervez liked him because he always shared an apple or pear or nectarine wrapped in white paper. One morning I heard him telling Mr. Pervez, "This city is losing its soul." Mr. Pervez liked this sort of talk too, about souls and spirits and ugly modern things.

Costanza's question made me realize for the first time that these customers always came by themselves. They all seemed old and lonely, without friends and families, even though they sometimes mentioned that a cheap little item reminded them of this or that person. Anyway, I told Costanza that there were always the same people in the shop, and he said I should let him know if I noticed anyone new. I think this was the first visit he had not mentioned his mountain.

Maybe Costanza had some sort of special spider sense or something because just such a person came into the store a few days after our conversation. He had been waiting outside in his buttoned-up coat and plaid hat. The minute I opened the door, he followed me inside. I saw him staring at the signed paintings of boats and lighthouses and farmhouses before he moved to the wooden chests, which he opened one by one. He was better dressed than the usual customers, and brisker too. I left the counter and followed him, though at a safe distance as I had been advised by Mr. Pervez. Since he seemed to be examining all sorts of items, I asked if he needed any assistance.

"What's the cost of this pipe?"

"It is twenty-five dollars, sir. It's very old."

"Yes, I can see that." He passed a finger over the cracks on the long curving stem. "And the machete on the wall? Where did you get such an item?"

Mr. Pervez had warned me to never mention the garage sales or places like the Salvation Army and the Donation Centre. Say it is from auctions, he advised, forced upon grieving, suddenly penniless families. When I told the customer this, he glanced at me in surprise. "How old are you?"

"I am eighteen, sir."

"And the owner of the shop?"

"Fifty or sixty." All old people seemed the same age to me.

"Do you accompany him to these auctions?"

I felt he was setting a trap so I decided to cut the conversation short. "Mr. Pervez, the owner, is at the back. He will explain better. Should I get him for you?"

He smiled at this and I noticed that his front teeth were much whiter than the others. "I will take the "—he glanced around—"torque corkscrew bottle opener on the wall."

When I mentioned this bottle-opener man to Costanza the next day, he immediately unloaded a ton of questions. Describe this man to me. What was his purchase? Did he ask any unusual questions? Where was Mr. Pervez at the time? On and on he went.

I tried to answer his questions as best as I could. I mentioned the machete and the corkscrew. Costanza took off his gloves, blew on his palms and examined his nails. He seemed extremely worried. I tried to cheer him up by pointing to a recently arrived crate crammed with rusty routers and drill bits, but he would have none of it.

"How long have you been working here, boy?"

"A year and a half." This is the week for questions, I thought.

"And before that?"

"I was in school."

"And before?"

"I lived in Trinidad. My father sent for me when I was sixteen after my mother died in Trinidad. I told you all of this before." I didn't like to talk about being all alone in our little basement apartment on Ellesmere for weeks on end, wondering when my father would return.

Maybe Costanza was surprised by my impatience for he now spoke in a softer voice. "Sammy...is that your name?"

"Samuel."

"Okay, Samuel then. I am more than three times your age. Do you believe that?"

I felt he may have been younger but I said nothing.

He was still gazing at the people walking by on Albert Street. "Look at these people outside. Moving at the same speed day after day. Now tell me... have you ever asked yourself where they are going?"

"They seem to be going to their jobs."

"Excellent. Excellent." He acted as if I had solved some difficult riddle. "I have another question. Have you ever noticed that their expressions never change from day to day?" In spite of his earlier annoyance he seemed to be enjoying this a bit. "Look at that woman with the shopping bags. Her face is as flat as a powder puff. A powder puff."

"They seem busy to me. In a hurry."

"Yes, yes. Very good. Busy running away."

"I didn't say that." After a while I asked him, "Running away from what?"

"From what they have left behind, Samuel. All of them have something dragging behind them. Sometimes the rope is a mile long and sometimes it is just a few inches. But the important thing, Samuel, is that just when they are beginning to forget, they feel the pull."

I said lightly: "You will need a real thick rope to pull a mountain?"

He smiled his sad faraway smile. "It is only when they are alone and safe in their little apartments...their little apartments, that the knot loosens."

After work that night, I squeezed in the subway car with a group of tired men and women. I sat between a small Chinese man and a woman who smelled of bleach or ammonia. They both slept until Victoria Park Station and after they had trudged off I wondered what they were dragging behind them to their tiny apartments.

• • •

The well-dressed man never returned, but early one morning, a pretty woman with a briefcase entered the store. She was not wearing a coat or anything heavy, but two silky layers that repeated the shape of her body. In a friendly voice, she asked if people actually bought all the old furniture and comic books and rusty tools. I followed her gaze over the shop and saw how it could be seen as junk, though the word she used was bric-a-brac. I wanted to impress her so I boasted of all our regular customers. She looked toward the office and asked if I had ever noticed any customers who came regularly without making any purchases. I shook my head. Then she wanted to know if Mr. Pervez had any regular visitors. I should have been suspicious of her but she was so pretty in her brown boots and skirt and deep red shirt that I wished I could tell her something she didn't know. All I could think of was that Mr. Pervez remained in his office most of the day. When she asked whether he was shy or perhaps hiding from someone, I remembered some of the annoyed customers who brought back items like knives and ugly statues and clay decanters that had been recently made in China, not years ago in Mexico or Brazil as Mr. Pervez had claimed. I didn't want to go into all of that, so I just told the lady, "Maybe." She gave me a nice smile and left.

I think it was a mistake to mention this lady to Costanza during his next visit. I shouldn't have brought up her question about regular customers. Maybe I wanted to show off about chatting with such a beautiful woman. Costanza grasped his umbrella and seemed prepared to leave, but at the doorway he hesitated and returned to the counter, walking very slowly. "I cannot blame you, Samuel. It was bound to happen. Don't feel too bad about it."

"About what? I am not feeling bad about anything."

He continued as if he had not heard me. "A man cannot run from his past, Samuel. He is tied to it, always, always." He squinted a bit and I was sure I had heard the line before in a western. He even looked a bit like Peter Ustinov from the old-time detective movies, smart and scheming. "Sadly my time is up. The noose is tighter than ever." He brushed his finger over his neck.

I think I was becoming a bit impatient with this mysterious sort of behaviour so I told him. "My time is up, too. I have to clean the store before I close. Mr. Pervez is away today." But Costanza made no attempt to leave; he just stood before me leaning on his umbrella. I have to say that I was glad he didn't walk away because for the next half an hour he finally explained the hold of his mountain. I cannot remember all of his exact words so I will try to fill in as best as I can.

Before he fled to Canada, he lived in some South American country, Peru or Chile, I cannot remember exactly. His family owned a huge plantation and he was always attended by servants. These servants were all tribal people and he remembered treating them, in the fashion of his parents, rather badly. Then he fell in love with one of these servants, a woman with dark striking eyes. He visited her often, without his family knowing. She lived in the mountains and he soon grew familiar with the people there and the secret tracks they had used for centuries.

"It is impossible to properly describe the ridges and breaks and gullies in the mountain, Samuel. The angle of the trees and the sprinkle of leaves. The colours and fragrance of the flowers. The land beneath so far away and the sky so close. There is a purity up there that you can never find anywhere else. It is so quiet that if you listen carefully you can hear the clouds moving. Brushing the peaks." He took one of his deep breaths and I wondered whether he was imitating some habit of his time there. "I cannot describe the people I grew to know so well. I used to pretend they were cloud people but as I became more familiar with them, I discovered a sad truth. A sad truth." He took another deep breath. "You see, Samuel, they were really plain people who many, many years earlier had been chased up the mountains by the rich cattle ranchers. Ranchers like my own family."

Now that I think of it, there were parts of Costanza'a story that were unsatisfactory. Maybe he couldn't remember everything or perhaps he did not want to reveal too much. Like the part where his parents found out about his mountain girlfriend and shipped him off to a university in another city. Or how easily he forgot about her while he escorted dozens of other women to parties and functions. He even found a job in this new city and got married.

"I believe it was three years into my unlucky marriage when my new, wealthy friends began to whisper nervously about the mountain tribes. They talked like scared little children about weapons bought from drug money, and guerrillas from neighbouring countries, and training camps and rebel bases deep in the mountains. I had little time for this nonsense, but then one night a ranch in my family's village was burned and its occupants murdered. Then it spread."

He paused and stared down at his umbrella as if he was trying to remember some small detail of that time. "At first, I was worried about my parents, as every good son should. But as the trouble spread, I began to think, more and more, of the mountain people I had grown to know. And about the woman I had left there. One night there was an argument." The quarrel was with his wife. He couldn't remember what the disagreement was about but believed it was pointless. "Something simple. Simple." The next morning he packed his bags.

This was the most puzzling part of his story. He didn't explain how he got caught up in the rebels' movement or how, after two years in the mountain, he became one of the leaders of the rebellion. They regularly ambushed the ragtag (his word) army and assassinated local government officials but they soon turned their sights on the president. (Or maybe the prime minister, I cannot remember exactly.) A plan was hatched. It included cooperative palace guards. Costanza was part of the squad that included five other men. Three of these men were killed, and two captured. Costanza and the other prisoner, an ordinary peasant, escaped but they lost each other in some swampy jungle. He felt for sure that the guards had set up the squad. "I can't tell you how many times I was almost captured," he told me, "before I came here to Canada." He pushed his umbrella beneath his arm and bowed like an actor in a play. "So here I am. Costanza, the refugee. Standing before you like an ordinary man."

"Is this your real name?"

"It's good as any. I have grown used to it."

I asked the question that was on my mind during the conclusion of his story. "And the woman?"

He took his umbrella and pointed it upwards, either at the sky or at his mountain.

"I am getting old. And the mountain is calling." He thrust out his hand. "Goodbye, Samuel. Goodbye. This may be the last time we meet."

♦ ♦ ♦

Costanza was right. I never saw him again.

I cannot say whether he heeded the call of the mountain or whether he was deported or captured, or continued living at his old address—wherever that was—laughing at the story he had pushed on to me. Maybe he still walks along Albert Street and stops at the intersection where Mr. Pervez's antique shop once stood. I still think of him and of his suspicions of the pretty questioning woman and the man who had bought the corkscrew. I can never be sure if they were there to investigate Mr. Pervez, whose simple little driving accident led to a background check and the discovery that he had been involved with some nasty group before his arrival in Canada. Anyways, to cut a long story short, Mr. Pervez was forced to close his shop, and although in those last days, he quarrelled endlessly about his bad luck, he never once blamed me for being so friendly with the pretty woman, or even waiting an entire week before I confessed my part in his distress. "Such is life," he had told me, speaking with the same sad faraway voice as Costanza when he said "a man is tied to his past, Sammy."

Sometimes when I am alone in my father's apartment, my mind moves into all sort of strange directions and I imagine Costanza and Pervez together, walking through swamps and up mountains and getting lost and always finding each other.

• • •

I now work nights at a video rental shop. A few nights ago I got off at the Victoria Park station and followed the woman who always smelled of bleach and ammonia. She stopped at a park in Jackson Street that was overshadowed by an old high rise. She sat on a bench and swung her stubby feet at the scattered leaves. She seemed in no hurry to get to her home. I stood behind a tree, some distance away. A runner gave me a nasty look so I moved from the shadow of the tree to a bench. The woman stopped her kicking and rested her head on the backrest of the bench. She remained like that for maybe half an hour, as if she was taking a little nap. Then she got up and dragged her bag up from the ground and slung it on her shoulder. The little rest must have done her good because her body didn't crumble as before, from the weight of the heavy bag. I watched her walking to the apartment and with each step she seemed straighter, so by the time she opened the glass door to the ground floor, she was looking like a much younger woman, maybe a pretty subway girl with a fashionable shawl hiding her neck. I remained on the bench until I saw the lights on a fourth floor apartment switch on. Costanza had told me that the knot would loosen only when they were alone and safe in their apartments. But on the balcony of this apartment was a row of Christmas lights, maybe left there from the last season. I felt there were many little children there, waiting patiently. As I walked away, I wondered when my father would return to our apartment in Ellesmere.

CONTRIBUTORS

DENISE BARNARD has published fiction in a variety of literary journals, including *Prairie Fire, The New Quarterly, Pagitica, McGill Street* and *White Wall Review,* as well as in *SightLines 8 Anthology,* a Grade Eight language arts anthology used in schools across Canada. In 2001, she attended The Banff Centre's Wired Writing Studio and is currently at work on a collection of interlinked short stories that includes "Caribana." Her first play, *This Life,* premiered at SummerWorks Theatre Festival in Toronto in 2002. Barnard is a freelance magazine editor who works with *Style at Home* magazine, and has also published in *The Globe and Mail.* She lives in Toronto.

MICHELE CHAI is an emerging writer and photographer who currently lives, dreams and agitates in Toronto. She is a Butch, Chinese-Trinidadian Feminist Warrior Dyke inspired by social justice movements and everyday acts of resistance. Her works endeavour to provoke conversation and action that build relationships and challenge accepted notions of sexuality, community and identity. Chai has been reading her poetry and short stories at Toronto venues and events since 1991. Her poetry has been published in the *Fireweed* issue subtitled "Rice Papers: Writings and Artwork by East and South East Asian Women," *Miscegenation Blues: Voices of Mixed Race Women,* edited by Carol Camper, and *Piece of My Heart: A Lesbian of Colour Anthology,* edited by Makeda Silvera.

NATASHA GILL was born in London, England, to a Trinidadian mother and a Pakistani father. The interesting cultural mix continued when the family moved to Canada in the late 1970s and she experienced growing up in suburban Mississauga. Gill has always loved to write and decided to go to journalism school at Carleton University after she realized her first career choice, commercial pilot, required some understanding of math and physics. She is currently pursuing a post-graduate degree in international development. She has worked and interned at Global Television, Reuters New Agency, the *Toronto Star* and the Discovery Channel's flagship daily science news show, *@discovery.ca*. An avid traveller, Gill loves to tell stories about the places, people and adventures she's had all over the world. "Potatoes Cause Brain Tumours" is based on stories her father used to tell her about growing up in a tiny Christian village in Pakistan.

MARLENE GOLDMAN lives and writes in Toronto. She is the author of short stories, poetry and plays. Her most recent poetry collection, *Shelter*, is under consideration by Pedlar Press, and she has embarked on another manuscript entitled *The Cook Not Mad*.

CATHERINE HERNANDEZ is a writer and theatre practitioner. She is the associate editor of Sweetmama.ca, was a columnist for the *National Post* and contributes to countless other publications. As the former head of Factory Theatre's Education/Outreach/Publicity program, she developed several strategies to increase the diversity of the theatre's audience and presented these tactics as a panellist at City Summit 2007. Her play *Singkil* premiered as part of Factory Theatre's 2006/07 season and was produced by fu-GEN Asian Canadian Theatre Company. *Singkil* and "Saint Candice" are in a several-part anthology-in-the-works called *The Scarborough Stories*, which includes *Kilt Pins* (a play about sexuality in a Catholic high school) and "Jude" (a short story about a champion bowler with a taste for married women). Hernandez now works as the marketing and development director for Native Earth Performing Arts and loves it.

LAWRENCE HILL's novels and non-fiction have been published to critical acclaim and have captured the interest and allegiance of readers across Canada. Among his recent work is the bestselling novel, *The Book of Negroes*. Hill is the child of a black father and a white mother who came to Canada hoping to escape the enduring racism of their native United States. Growing up in the predominantly white suburb of Don Mills, Ontario, in the 1060s, Hill was greatly influenced by his parents' work in the human rights movement. Much of his writing touches on issues of identity and race.

RABINDRANATH MAHARAJ is the author of *A Perfect Pledge*, which was shortlisted for a Regional Commonwealth Writers' Prize and the Rogers Writers'

Trust Fiction Award, *The Lagahoo's Apprentice*, which was listed as a notable book of the year by both *The Globe and Mail* and the *Toronto Star*, and *Homer in Flight*, which was nominated for the Chapters/Books in Canada First Novel Award. He is also the author of two collections of short stories, *The Book of Ifs and Buts* and *The Interloper*, which was nominated for a Regional Commonwealth Prize for Best First Book. Maharaj was born in Trinidad and now lives in Ajax, Ontario. He was recently the Writer in Residence at the Toronto Reference Library, and is an instructor at the Humber School for Writers. He was one of the founders of the literary magazine *Lichen*.

IAN MALCZEWSKI is a Toronto-based writer who has lived in Montreal and Melbourne, Australia. He recently completed a degree in English and semiotics at the University of Toronto, and is toying with the idea of graduate school in the near future. He occasionally writes for *Spacing Magazine* on Toronto waterfront issues and contributes a weekly column about the "poetry" of Toronto public space landmarks for the Toronto website, blogTO. He also performs in the community musical group Samba Elegua, an organization that has been bringing amateur activism and rump-shaking fun to the streets for over five years.

FERESHTEH MOLAVI, an Iranian native, is a bibliographer and scholar, as well as a freelance editor and translator. While still living in Iran, she published articles and books, among them a novel, *The House of Cloud and Wind* (1991), and a collection of short stories, *The Sun Fairy* (1991). *Listen to the Reed*, a chapbook published by PEN Canada in 2005, is based on her dialogue with Karen Connelly. Molavi has been included in anthologies, including *Afsaneh: Short Stories by Iranian Women* (2005) and *Speaking in Tongues: PEN Canada Writers in Exile* (2005). Her stories and essays have been published in various Persian magazines and anthologies, and she has held readings in Sweden, the United States and Canada. Her new collection of short stories in Persian, *The Wandering Nightingale*, was released in Tehran in 2005. A member of PEN Canada, Molavi has joined the Scholars-at-Risk Program at Massey College in 2006 and currently teaches Persian literature at the University of Toronto. Her first collection of short stories in English will be released by Luna Publications in fall 2007.

NERMEEN MOUFTAH was born and raised in Kingston, Ontario, and moved to Toronto to study English and political science at the University of Toronto. She continued her study of literature at University College London. Her poetry, short fiction and photography have appeared in journals in Canada and the United Kingdom. She has taught English as a second language as well as English literature and is currently working on a Canadian International Development Agency project in Cairo.

EVAN PLACEY is a graduate of McGill University and the University of London in England. He is a poet and playwright whose plays include *Caffeine, Saturday in the Aisles, Phone Play, Fragments of Us* and *Dinner on the Fourteenth Floor.* Currently in development are *Snow Falls on the Oublie Trees* and *White Other.* His plays have been performed in Toronto, Montreal, Edinburgh and London. He is the recipient of the Clark Lewis Prize and the Lionel Shapiro Award for Creative Writing. Placey continues to write, produce and direct new work in both Canada and the United Kingdom.

DOLLY REISMAN recently finished her first novel, is working on a book of short stories and is workshopping a play about Albert Speer, Hitler's architect. She is currently developing a documentary on the topic of love. She is also co-producer of Yiddish Speak, a video archive of Yiddish speakers. She has written scripts for several films, including *The Baby Game* and *Angel Light,* as well as *Walk Foot Man,* which won a Silver Medal at the Chicago Film Festival. Reisman's theatre writing credits include *Mr. Nice Guy,* co-written with Tom Walmsley and performed at the Toronto Free Theatre; *Nothing But the Truth,* co-written with Judy Silver to promote racial tolerance; *Girls Can Boys Can,* which toured Ontario; and the two-woman show *Skin and Bones* for the Edmonton Fringe Festival, which she both wrote and produced.

KERRI SAKAMOTO is a Toronto-based writer of novels, screenplays and essays on visual art. Her first novel, *The Electrical Field,* received the Commonwealth Prize for Best First Book and the Canada-Japan Literary Award, and was short-listed for several other honours. It and her second novel, *One Hundred Million Hearts,* have been published in translation internationally. She is presently at work on a third novel for which she received a Chalmers Fellowship. She is the Barker Fairley Distinguished Visitor in Canadian Studies at University College at the University of Toronto (2005–2007).

DEVYANI SALTZMAN was born in Toronto. She received a degree in human sciences from Oxford University, specializing in sociology and anthropology. *Shooting Water,* published by Key Porter Books in 2005, received starred reviews in both *Publishers Weekly* and *Library Journal* and has been published internationally. Her writing has also appeared in *The Globe and Mail, Marie Claire* and is upcoming in *The Walrus.*

TASLEEM THAWAR was born in North York and grew up in Unionville. Since then, she has lived and worked in Japan, India, England and Tanzania. Thawar has recently moved back to Toronto, and is excited to be living above ground, under slanted ceilings.

PRISCILA UPPAL is a poet and fiction writer born in Ottawa and currently living in Toronto. Among her publications are five collections of poetry: *How to Draw Blood from a Stone* (1998), *Confessions of a Fertility Expert* (1999), *Pretending to Die* (2001), *Live Coverage* (2003) and *Ontological Necessities* (2006), all published by Exile Editions. She has also written the novel *The Divine Economy of Salvation* (2002), published to critical acclaim by Doubleday Canada and Algonquin Books of Chapel Hill and translated into Dutch and Greek. Her poetry has been translated into Korean, Croatian, Latvian and Italian, and *Ontological Necessities* was short-listed for the prestigious Griffin Prize for Excellence in Poetry in 2007. She has a PhD in English literature and is a professor of humanities and English at York University and coordinator of the university's Creative Writing Program.

GEIN WONG is a writer and electronic music composer who weaves emotion and power into her works. She has performed across Canada as well as in England, the United States, the Caribbean and East Asia. Her debut CD *Thousand Mile Voice* is a warm and distinctive blend of poetry, East Asian acoustic instruments and electronic brushed beats. Her work has been published in numerous literary journals, magazines, zines and anthologies, including the *Strong Words: Year Two, Ricepaper, Fireweed, Bamboo Girl* and *Strike the Wok: Chinese Canadian Prose*. Her piece "A Paper Son" appears on the *Dig Your Roots* Canadian spoken word CD. She is currently working on a novel that chronicles the early effects of capitalism and colonization on a community. As well, she is composing music for the dance company Little Pear Garden, the multimedia performance group the Movement Project and the music group the Fusilli Project. Wong is a proud and passionate co-founder and co-director of the Toronto Asian Arts Freedom School.

COVER ARTIST

Born in Seoul, Korea, in 1978, TEK moved to Canada in 2000. Before moving to Toronto, he served as a surveillance photographer for the South Korean Military and later in the Military Press. After arriving in Toronto, TEK attended George Brown College and later earned his BFA at the Ontario College of Art and Design. TEK's photo-based art has been shown in numerous galleries across Canada and collected by many corporations. In his spare time, TEK is an avid competitive cyclist and Korean gourmet chef. He currently works in one of Toronto's finest photo galleries and will be pursuing his MFA in near future.

About the cover images:
"Each day is filled with a sameness that blinds us to the moments that are unique. We grab a coffee, see the same streetscapes, exchange the same jokes, focusing on what is the same. This provides a sense of security and predictability that we think is *good*. We call our view 'reality' but everywhere around us, everything and everyone is changing. Each day, we walk through our lives with a choice: we can tune out along our road to more of the same, or we can open our eyes to change and live. It is all in our path."

www.gallerytek.com

Diaspora
Dialogues

Diaspora Dialogues supports the creation and presentation of
new fiction, poetry and drama that reflect the complexity
of Toronto back to Torontonians through the eyes of its richly
diverse communities.

For information on our publishing and mentoring programs,
or on our monthly multidisciplinary performance series,
please visit www.diasporadialogues.com or call 416 944 1101.

Diaspora Dialogues gratefully acknowledges the support of
The Maytree Foundation, Ontario Trillium Foundation,
Heritage Canada and the Government of Canada through the
Book Publishing Industry Development Program and of the
City of Toronto through the Toronto Arts Council.